TRIGGER™
The voice of mental health

The**inspirational**series™
Overcoming adversity and thriving

Beautif... Ch... 5

A... ...ipolar

We are pro... ...onalseries™. Part of the Trigg... ...novative mental health books, The**inspirational**series™ tells the stories of the people who have battled and beaten mental health issues. For more information visit: www.triggerpublishing.com

THE AUTHOR

After 35 years of battling serious mental illness, Ali was eventually diagnosed with bipolar disorder II.

An established television presenter for more than 20 years, Ali presented the national news, made history by becoming the first woman to present football's Scottish Premier League, and featured in countless newspapers and magazines.

Despite her outwardly glamorous and showbiz lifestyle, Ali was secretly fighting wild mood swings and devastating depression. At her lowest point, she came dangerously close to ending her life.

Holding down such a high-pressure job in the public eye, along with her everyday fight against bipolar, took its toll, and she turned to drugs and alcohol as an escape. On eventually receiving an accurate diagnosis, Ali's life changed beyond recognition.

Since her diagnosis, Ali has forged a new life for herself, with her boyfriend, "Handsome Doc" and her son, MK.

First published in Great Britain 2018 by Trigger

Trigger is a trading style of Shaw Callaghan Ltd & Shaw Callaghan 23 USA, INC.

The Foundation Centre

Navigation House, 48 Millgate, Newark

Nottinghamshire NG24 4TS UK

www.triggerpublishing.com

Copyright © Ali Douglas 2018

British Library Cataloguing in Publication Data

A CIP catalogue record for this book is available upon request
from the British Library

ISBN: 978-1-78956-006-0

This book is also available in the following e-Book and Audio formats:

MOBI: 978-1-78956-009-1
EPUB: 978-1-78956-007-7
PDF: 978-1-78956-008-4
AUDIO: 978-1-78956-010-7

Ali Douglas has asserted her right under the Copyright,
Design and Patents Act 1988 to be identified as the author of this work

Cover design and typeset by Fusion Graphic Design Ltd

Printed and bound in Great Britain by Clays Ltd, Elcograf S.p.A

Paper from responsible sources

www.triggerpublishing.com

Thank you for purchasing this book.
You are making an incredible difference.

Proceeds from all Trigger books go directly to
The Shaw Mind Foundation, a global charity that focuses
entirely on mental health. To find out more about
The Shaw Mind Foundation visit,
www.shawmindfoundation.org

MISSION STATEMENT

Our goal is to make help and support available for every
single person in society, from all walks of life.
We will never stop offering hope. These are our promises.

Trigger and The Shaw Mind Foundation

A NOTE FROM THE SERIES EDITOR

The Inspirational range from Trigger brings you genuine stories about our authors' experiences with mental health problems.

Some of the stories in our Inspirational range will move you to tears. Some will make you laugh. Some will make you feel angry, or surprised, or uplifted. Hopefully they will all change the way you see mental health problems.

These are stories we can all relate to and engage with. Stories of people experiencing mental health difficulties and finding their own ways to overcome them with dignity, humour, perseverance and spirit.

Ali Douglas' story is a powerful one that details her life with bipolar disorder II. She writes candidly about how her television career was affected by her mental health difficulties, and how she abused alcohol and drugs as an unhelpful coping strategy. Ali provides unique insight into what is like to live with bipolar II disorder, a disorder that is frequently misdiagnosed and misunderstood. Ali's journey through her mental health challenges is harrowing and at times devastating, but her strength shines through in her words as does her determination to educate others by sharing her experiences.

This is our Inspirational range. These are our stories. We hope you enjoy them. And most of all, we hope that they will educate and inspire you. That's what this range is all about.

Lauren Callaghan,
Co-founder and Lead Consultant Psychologist at Trigger

I'm strong, because I've been weak. I'm fearless, because I've been afraid. I'm wise, because I've been foolish.

Author unknown

Disclaimer: Some names and identifying details have been changed to protect the privacy of individuals.

PREFACE

Compared to other health problems, many mental illnesses remain misunderstood, and are badly affected by stigma; none more so than bipolar.

A not uncommon perception is that bipolar is nothing more than a cool label for people experiencing ups and downs.

I'd be delighted to have the illness if that were the case. Bring it on! I'd happily put down my money for a job lot of fitted V-neck T-shirts with 'Bipolar Rocks' emblazoned on them, so that everyone would know how cool I really am.

Then there are the people who say, 'But you don't look depressed. You're always so happy!'

I get that. I don't think it's fair to blame people who simply don't know about mental illness. It's a minefield even for those of us who live with it!

Here's the thing though. I'm no expert in asthma. But I'm willing to learn. And crucially, in the meantime, I don't judge.

My all-time favourite interpretation of what it is to be bipolar came from a well-meaning nurse of all people. I was in hospital for a minor procedure. It wasn't related to bipolar, but as it happened, I was in the throes of a dark depression.

A very sweet Irish nurse, who looked as though her retirement party may well be in the planning phase, knew my medical history ... and wanted to cure me. Of bipolar.

She meant well.

As I lay sobbing on the hospital trolley, unable to utter a word, wondering how long this latest depressive episode would last, this sweet Irish nurse patted my cannula-decorated hand (a bit too hard), and assured me that there was no need for me to be depressed.

Jolly good! Wish someone had told me that sooner.

'It's a waste of your God-given energy,' she went on. 'A young girl like you should be out enjoying herself, not lying here crying over something or nothing.'

She hadn't finished.

'Now listen dear. There's nothing a cup of herbal tea can't fix and you're in luck. They filled up the staffroom cupboard this morning. Will lemon and ginger do you?'

Sadly, the lemon and ginger tea didn't magic away my mental illness.

The hard facts are these:

- Bipolar increases your risk of suicide by 20 times.
- Up to half of bipolar sufferers will attempt suicide at least once.

It's not cool, it's not fashionable, and it's not a fad.

Bipolar is a severe mental illness characterised by extreme mood swings, known as manic highs and depressive lows.

It can affect anyone, and is thought to be caused by chemical imbalances in the brain.

It's also thought that there's a genetic link. Children of a parent with bipolar are 10 to 15 per cent more likely to develop it.

Again. Not so cool.

The good news, though, is that like all supposedly cool accessories, the illness comes in different varieties. There's no "one size fits all" with this fashion must-have.

I don't mean to make light. This is an extremely serious illness, but I wouldn't have reached the place I'm at in my life now without a sense of humour.

I live with bipolar II, where the highs are known as "hypomania". These episodes don't cause hallucinations or psychosis, but they can be so debilitating that it's impossible to function in day-to-day life. The lows are just as severe as those associated with bipolar I.

As yet, there is no known cure for the illness, and even when I'm in a good and stable place, I'm never allowed to forget that I'm clinically bipolar. There's still a darkness in my peripheral vision.

Nevertheless, I truly believe it's possible to carve out something resembling a meaningful life with bipolar. There have been times in my life when it has only been a very vague resemblance to a "normal" life, but other times when it's been a pretty convincing body double. And we're so strong! Like other people who have experienced mental illness, I have learnt to fight for my health every single day. As a community of people, I believe we develop an intrinsic strength, and have great wells of stamina and courage to draw upon.

Couple that with the right medical support, and you can minimise the mood swings significantly – assuming you get diagnosed correctly of course.

Assuming you get diagnosed at all ...

PART I
1974 – 2009
UNDIAGNOSED CHAOS

CHAPTER 1

STEPPING OUT OF THE SEA

It happened while I was on holiday in Spain with my older sister and her family.

I was standing knee-deep in the sea, on a beautiful deserted beach, with the waves lapping the shore as the sun went down.

I must have looked like someone who hadn't a care in the world. Like someone who was soaking up the peace and serenity of her surroundings, before heading home for some tapas and a glass of Sangria.

Nothing could have been further from the truth. I was 27 years old and was preparing to kill myself.

I'd planned it all out in advance.

I was going to take a whole heap of Valium and wade out into the sea until it became so deep that I'd need to swim. Then swim as far as I possibly could, until exhaustion and the effects of the Valium kicked in, and I couldn't swim any longer.

I wanted to drown. I wanted to die.

This latest bout of depression had caused such excruciating mental and physical torture that suicide seemed like the only option I had left.

I wanted to sink into a beautiful oblivion. To stop the pain. To stop the agonising loneliness and feelings of utter uselessness.

I wanted to stop the never-ending flow of tears.

To be free. To be light.

I played with the bottle of Valium in my hand. Ironic really that they have a child tamper-proof opening. What about a tamper-proof opening for suicidal depressives wanting to overdose?

As I stood in the sea for what seemed like hours, I watched the sun disappear, and the warm glow of the day bid me farewell. For the last time.

Gradually, I waded in a little deeper until the water was skimming the bottom of my denim cut-offs.

So many thoughts were going through my head. It wasn't that my mind was racing, more like it was turning over every last thought very slowly, and rationally, or so it seemed at the time.

What would it actually feel like?

Was drowning really the quick and silent death that my research had told me it was?

Would my lungs take in enough water to make me unconscious and allow nature to take its course?

I had battled with an undiagnosed mental illness for as long as I could remember, and I'd developed a strength and an inner fight. Did that mean instinct would kick in, and I'd find myself fighting for survival?

That's what the Valium was for. I knew that, if I took enough of it, it would induce a happy, drunk feeling before I fell into a coma. I knew this because I'd spent hours researching how I was going to kill myself in minute detail.

To this day, and all these years later, my eyes still fill up when I recount the events of that evening.

I never did take the Valium and I didn't wade out into the sea.

Instead, I turned around and waded in the opposite direction until I reached the beach, where I collapsed onto the cool sand, crying uncontrollably.

As I lay there, I went through spells of silent agony. The tears tumbled down my face, but I couldn't utter a sound. At other times, I wailed. I wailed and sobbed and hugged my knees for comfort, searching for any kind of relief from the desperate sadness I was feeling.

So, what made me turn around and return to the shore?

My family.

The overriding image was that of my family being in bits.

Of my mum sobbing. Of her soul enduring torture so unbearably painful that she would physically hurt. The image is almost too much to bear.

I knew that Mum and Dad would never get over the pain of losing me. They live for their three girls. Life would have ended for them that day.

In time, they would have gathered all the strength they could muster to try to prop up my sisters. To bear their pain. But none of them would have lived again.

I already felt like I was a burden to them, but to do this would have utterly destroyed them.

My poor, poor, sister would never have known where I had gone, or what had become of me. Eventually, she would have had to get on the plane home without me.

The Valium ended up in the sea, but I didn't.

When I returned to the villa, my sister, her husband and the children were still playing in the pool. Despite my puffy eyes, I managed to arrange my face into a big smile. I told them that I'd had a lovely walk, before asking what their plans were for supper.

I still find it hard to comprehend just how close I came to taking my own life. How close I came to shattering the lives of so many people.

As I sit here today tapping away on my laptop, yes there are tears, but I also feel an enormous sense of gratitude.

Gratitude, would you believe, to my mental illness, although it was still undiagnosed at that time.

Every day of my life had been a battle to some degree or another. As a result, I had built up an almost subconscious resilience to win my battles against depression. But now the stakes were higher than they'd ever been before.

We went out for supper that evening. Tapas and a glass of Sangria. For a brief moment, with my family again, I was at peace. How long it would last for I couldn't possibly know. But in that moment, there was peace.

The following day we flew home. Home to face the next round in the ring, knowing that the darkness would descend again. And feeling like it would never, ever stop.

CHAPTER 2

THE GREMLIN IS BORN

Childhood should be a time of innocence and inquisitiveness.

Your only stress or worry should be whether or not you'll be able to persuade your mum to give you spaghetti hoops with your tea instead of broccoli.

Childhood should be joyful and carefree. Your time should be spent learning to ride a bike without stabilisers, and playing hide-and-seek with your grandpa ...

Ironically, I was able to ride my bike without stabilisers easily enough, but these days, I'm unable to ride the waves of everyday life without stabilisers of a different type. Thank you, mood stabiliser pills, you really do pull your weight.

From as far back as I can remember, I've been an all-or-nothing kind of a girl.

I think deeply. I feel strongly. My mind used to be a constant whirlwind of emotion, and I invested everything into whatever the obsession of the moment happened to be.

This is still the case today, but to a much lesser extent.

None of this is to say I had a miserable childhood. I'm the middle child of three girls, and was brought up in a house where love was on tap, with parents who did their level best to provide a fulfilling childhood for us.

My elder sister and I were obsessed with horses, and were lucky enough to have our own handsome little Connemara pony called Doric.

Our summer holiday was a fortnight in Arran, a small island off the west coast of Scotland. It was a happy time, spent playing with our cousins, having barbecues on the beach, (invariably in the rain), and fishing for crabs off the end of the pier.

Incidentally, we'd return the crabs unharmed each night, only to catch the same ones the following night. The crabs got to have a little adventure and got a free meal of our bait thrown in for their troubles!

Mum and Dad are good people. They make me want to be a better person. They are very involved with the church, and it seems to me like they do more charity work than Mother Teresa!

They read for the blind and Mum donates platelets every few weeks. They both spend entire nights at the homeless mission, offering support to vulnerable and disadvantaged people. They stand in Glasgow on cold November days, selling poppies to commemorate ex-servicemen and women.

They visit the lonely and elderly, giving the benefits of their time and their light-hearted chat. They help local refugees integrate into society. In fact, they recently invited a family to their home for a barbecue. The gesture was reciprocated, with Mum and Dad being invited back to their home for supper which humbled them greatly.

I could go on, but you get the picture.

What I admire the most, though, is that they do it all quietly. They tell no one of their good work, as they don't want to appear too saintly or self-righteous. Even I have to push them to get the details of what they've been up to!

Aside from being good and kind people, they are great fun. They have a wonderful circle of close friends and an active social life.

The point is – I aspire to be more like them.

So, with all that in mind, it's no surprise that I had an intrinsically lovely childhood. Despite the chaos going on in my head, I'll always be grateful for the many happy times.

On the face of it, we were a tight, well-balanced, little family unit. But the turmoil in my head was developing all the time.

And then, one day, the "gremlin" was born.

As it turns out, he wasn't just passing through either. He was honing his skills on how best to declare war on my unarmed mind, and he somehow managed to earn himself squatter's rights. To this day, no one has been able to evict him.

Incidentally, the gremlin isn't a voice in my head. The gremlin is the name I give to the imbalance in my brain which causes my mental illness.

I've never actually heard the gremlin. He doesn't speak to me as such. He just lurks in my mind, and leaps out whenever he fancies wreaking a bit of havoc.

He was first named years ago, during a conversation with Mum. I was in my teens, and she was hugging me after we'd had a set-to. She said something about that little gremlin in my head causing trouble again.

It stuck. We've referred to the gremlin ever since. He is the catalyst for my extreme behaviour.

Looking back on it, my mental health has probably never been great.

Even when I was four or five, I can remember feeling a real sense of social anxiety, mainly with anyone older than me. I was more comfortable with girls of my own age. Lots of little girls and boys feel embarrassed and shy at times. This was more than that, though.

I was incredibly sensitive, and having easily hurt feelings made fitting in very difficult. So, in turn, it became very difficult to create a bond with anyone. It was self-perpetuating too. I could see everyone else forming bonds, which just magnified the feelings of not being a part of something.

I had to let go but didn't know how.

For me, the saddest part of it all is that rather than try to explain what I didn't even understand myself, it was easier for me to say nothing at all. I believed that my voice was not valid. Had I spoken up and shared how I really felt in my troubled mind, people would have laughed at me.

They wouldn't have laughed.

Being silent meant feeling empty and lonely, but it also meant staying safe. By keeping quiet, I wasn't putting myself out there where I would have been ridiculed.

I wouldn't have been ridiculed.

I still don't know why, but when I was with older family friends or older cousins, all of whom were kind and inclusive, I cared far too much about what they thought of me. I'm sure they were thinking nothing at all. Why would they? Why would I convince myself that they were focusing on me? They were entirely accepting of me just as I was, but I felt as though I was constantly being judged.

I wasn't being judged at all.

My self-esteem was on the floor. I was entrenched in my own mind, and that was not a good place to be.

I was five years old! To be putting myself through such torment was just not right for someone so young.

Mum and Dad were aware of how awkward I used to feel. They gave me all the love and encouragement they could, to try to help me feel more comfortable in my skin. Mum used to be terribly shy when she was younger, and used to say that she wished she hadn't passed that down to me.

Poor Mum. I blame her for nothing. She's still my role model.

The real problems began to present a few years later though. By the age of eight or nine, it became clear that I had anger issues. And while every child feels frustration at being misunderstood, my agitated mind would cause me to implode.

This certainly didn't come from Mum. Or from Dad for that matter. It was a unique, and unwelcome, facet of my personality that I despised, and I didn't blame anyone else for it.

One Sunday morning, we were all getting ready to go to church. Correction: four members of the household were getting ready to go to church. The middle child sat stubbornly in her bedroom dressed in jodhpurs and a riding jacket.

I can remember fiddling around with the little silver horse brooch, pinned to my jacket, which I'd recently been given for my birthday.

I was fuming.

Church was at 11 o'clock, and I'd already aired my annoyance that it was, 'right in the middle of the day.' I'd been desperate to get out to the stables, for no particular reason, other than that I loved being with the horses.

Church was important to my parents though, so to them, it was irrelevant what time the service started. We were all going. And that was that. But the Sunday routine didn't stop at church. There was a full Sunday lunch to endure before I could escape to the stables.

Mum would put the chicken in the Aga first thing in the morning, so that it would be ready when we got home from church. Then the potatoes would need to be boiled, the vegetables would be prepared, and the bread sauce made.

All perfectly reasonable on my parents' part. They more than deserved their Sunday routine. On this particular day though, it seemed like the most infuriating waste of good horsey time.

When my protestations about the time of the church service had been brushed off, I stormed upstairs to my room yelling about how selfish my parents were. The irony!

But I didn't stop at that. I stomped into my room, slammed the door shut with such gusto that I'm surprised it didn't come off its hinges, and proceeded to pick up random objects and lob them against the wall.

I had completely lost it.

I ripped up my horse posters, sent alarm clocks flying, and dismembered Sindy doll's horses.

I was screaming, shouting, and crying inconsolably.

My brain had gone into lockdown, and it was jammed on the self-destruct setting.

It's excruciating to reveal this to you. Not just because it was such an inexplicable overreaction, but also because it was the kind of backlash you might expect from a three-year-old. Not a nine-year-old. It wasn't uncommon back then though. The least likely of disagreements could see me melt down faster than an ice lolly on a hot day. I became so incensed that I was completely unaware of my surroundings, completely unaware of my actions, and completely out of control.

By that stage, the initial reason for my anger was no longer on my mind. In fact, nothing was on my mind.

The pattern was always the same. After a few minutes, I would collapse in a heap on the floor sobbing, desperately wanting to be hugged.

It was always Dad I wanted. I needed him to hug me tightly and tell me that everything was okay, that it was all over, and that he and Mum loved me very much.

After that, I wouldn't have wanted to go to the stables even if they had let me. I just wanted to be with them. To feel safe and to be at peace. To be normal.

I always did get that hug in the end.

Mum and Dad tried several things to try to help me channel my uncontrollable rage.

Sometimes Dad would offer his upstretched palms for me to punch my frustrations away. That didn't go so well, though, when I accidentally punched his chunky gold wedding band with my fist.

Dad was fine, but my fist hurt like hell. This didn't please me one bit and did little to calm me down.

The next victim presented to me was a punch bag. A floor standing Smurfs inflatable punch bag.

It worked for a while, until I burst it with one thump too many. Turns out I had quite a good right hook.

The curious thing was that these episodes of anger only happened at home. Never outside the home. And although I had a terrible temper, it never came close to being directed at anyone. I detest violence against people. It upsets me hugely to see any type of physical violence, even on TV.

Sindy doll's plastic horses were living on borrowed time though.

In the aftermath of one of my epic meltdowns, Dad was trying to soothe me. He was stroking my forehead and telling me that everything would be okay.

I was hyperventilating. It took a while to reach a state of calm after these explosive episodes. And he said to me, 'Everything you do, you do to extremes.'

He was right.

I think I was off school on the day they taught the word "moderation".

Over and above my anger issues, I also displayed obsessive tendencies, and my moods were far more extreme than simply "excited" or "happy".

These moods generated the kind of behaviour you'd expect of an excitable jack-in-the-box on cocaine.

On one occasion, when I was eight, I cleaned and tidied my little Pierrot-decorated bedroom. Pierrot, of course, is the sad clown with the tear tumbling down his white face. So basically, this little girl with depressive tendencies had surrounded herself with sadness. Make of that what you will.

Now on reading this, it probably doesn't sound as though there's anything particularly weird about me blitzing my bedroom. Lots of little girls like a tidy room ...

The devil is in the detail though, and oh my days, these details were possessed.

I hauled everything out of the wardrobe, throwing it behind me so that I could clean every single millimetre of the unit itself. Those corners could get so dusty. And as for the rail? Enough said.

I turned to the clothes. I made sure my white school blouses were all hung in the white section of the colour-coded rail, and I buttoned up every single button to keep them neat and smooth.

I took out the shoes. They didn't need to be polished (but you can always achieve a little more shine with a good buff). Afterwards, there was still something bothering me. So, I set about re-lacing every single shoe so that the ends were exactly the same length.

Everything got the same treatment before being meticulously but speedily moved back into the spotlessly clean wardrobe.

The hangers were all spaced out evenly and facing the same way. That took a while, and required a lot of tweaking, but boy was it worth it.

Next came my Matilda doll set. I marched to and from the bathroom until I had moved every item of furniture from her house to the sink, ready to be washed. I used my facecloth to wash everything before drying and polishing it all using most of a roll of toilet paper. Finicky job given that Matilda's cutlery can't have been any more than three millimetres long.

I folded Matilda's clothes. I *always* folded Matilda's clothes, but there was always scope to get them just that little bit flatter and smoother.

I could have got a job in Gap, such was the standard of my folding.

I smoothed my Pierrot bedspread and pillowcase, and pulled them so straight and taut that they resembled a starched tablecloth at a Royal wedding at Buckingham Palace. Hospital corners abounded.

Teddy Eddie was precisely propped up against the pillow to ensure he was exactly central. He watched as I rushed around the room, frantically cleaning everything in sight, terrified I might miss something and end up living in squalor.

I was moving so fast. Racing through the tasks. It wasn't just my boundless energy. I wanted – no, I needed – to get it all done as quickly as possible so that I wouldn't be breathing in any more dirt.

My knicker drawer? Yeah, that was a little tricky. The *My Little Pony* knickers were a slightly different shape from the love heart ones. I tried several different approaches, but eventually plumped for a method of folding each pair back slightly at the side seam to create the illusion that they were all identical in shape. Pleased with that.

And so it went on.

I'd saved the best until last though.

Having already hoovered the carpet and used the suction tools to get into every single little edge or corner, I stood back to assess the way the room was shaping up.

On the face of it, it was okay. In fact, it was gleaming and would've sailed through inspection in an army barracks. It didn't look good to me though. There was still something seriously wrong ...

Although I had hoovered, I couldn't help thinking that I had only cleaned the surface of the carpet. What about underneath the pile? Why had I never thought of that before? There must be loads of manky matter lurking around in there.

Only one thing for it. I'd need to brush it out by hand using the nail brush. It was the only brush hard enough to get right in amongst the pile.

It was a painstaking job that took at least an hour and a half. It looked absolutely no different when I'd finished, but it made me feel a little calmer. It slowed my racing mind and heart.

This frenzied cleaning episode was typical of my Obsessive Compulsive Disorder (OCD) tendencies. They always came hand-in-hand with a high – it was as if my perception of reality became more heightened, and I felt things more acutely.

As I had looked around my bedroom at the beginning of that afternoon, I hadn't seen the tidiness that most people would have seen. I hadn't seen a room where everything was in its place. I had seen dirt and mess. I had seen germs. And there may even have been tiny little bugs hiding away in the carpet, for all I knew.

I had been horrified. Disgusted. There was absolutely no question that I could have just left it as it was.

If, for any reason, I hadn't been able to clean and tidy my Pierrot bedroom that day, I would have reached a state of anxiety beyond comprehension.

I would have been fidgety, snappy, incredibly impatient and intolerant. There would have been no way on earth that I could have settled down enough to do something else. I would have been frantically thinking up a way to get stuck into the cleaning. The thought of not giving into the cleaning frenzy would have been unthinkable. My parents could have put a padlock on the door and it wouldn't have stopped me. Somehow, I'd have found the strength to force the door down.

Once that seed had been planted, it would become the single most important thing in my life at that moment.

My OCD tendencies were not driven by choice. I was powerless to stop them; they were a desperate need that had to be satisfied.

Back then, my highs and lows were shorter lived than they became in the years to follow. So, it only took until that evening for the inevitable to happen ...

My mood crashed. Any signs of a happy, carefree, eight-year-old girl vanished. I became incredibly sad and heavy. I felt so lonely, despite the fact I was in a house occupied by four other people. I felt utterly worthless. I felt ugly and stupid next to my bright, beautiful sisters.

I had never felt confident about the way I looked. Far from it. But my feelings of self-loathing and insecurity next to my sisters were at their worst when the lows hit.

My sisters were (and are) nothing but lovely. Humble and self-depreciating, with good, kind hearts. They would have been so sad to know how I felt next to them.

As the low began to envelop me, it must've just seemed like I was tired. Not surprising given the energy I'd expended on the big clean. Back in those days, before we had given my gremlin a name, no one could have known that he was fiddling with my emotional dial, turning it right down, almost to the off position. It would be a long time until any of us knew what we were dealing with.

There was no pleading to stay up late that night. I was straight to bed at the first mention of it. But it took me ages to get to sleep. It wasn't that my mind was racing, more that I was being forced to endure the desperate sadness. I wasn't allowed to sleep; that would have meant escaping the pain. It would have meant peace from the whirlpool of thoughts swirling around my mind. And that would have seemed too easy.

Some of the thoughts I had were so outlandish that it's hard to believe they were the product of such a young girl.

I worried that I would never achieve perfection in anything, be it school grades or the way I rode my horse. It felt like I would always be chasing the impossible. My parents were so proud of me, yet I was setting them up for a fall.

I would fail all the "grown-up" exams at school so would never get a job. What would I do then? Would Mum and Dad need to look after me for the rest of my life?

I'd remain the ugly duckling that I had convinced myself I was, while my sisters continued to blossom into beautiful young women. I'd be the sister that people felt sorry for. The sister who had fallen by the wayside. The clumsy, geeky weirdo to whom nobody could relate.

Thinking like that wasn't just exhausting; it was debilitating.

The picture couldn't have been more different when I had a high. During these periods, I'd actually get excited about the cottage in the country I knew would have when I grew up.

It would be picture-perfect, complete with a white picket fence, and climbing white roses framing the door.

I'd be a three-time Olympic champion showjumper, and would count Virginia Leng (my childhood equestrian heroine) as a close friend.

I was eight. Eight years old and experiencing mood fluctuations that were beyond my comprehension. At that time, I never tried to figure out why it was happening. Why would I? It was just me. I was a weirdo.

I wasn't a weirdo.

All I knew was that I was either super excited, or as flat as a pancake. Little did I know that episodes like this were to mark a lifetime of turbulence. Of extreme behaviour.

Little did I know that the hypomanic episodes and depressive lows were going to cause such great pain to me and those close to me from then on in.

In the meantime though, it was time to don my armour and prepare for battle.

CHAPTER 3

GROWING PAINS

When people said, 'Schooldays are the best days of your life,' I always hoped that they were being ironic. If not, I didn't much fancy the shape of things to come.

At times, I found school really tough. Particularly my days at secondary school.

I was a funny mix though. (No breaking news there, then!)

By the time I reached secondary school, I had a great bunch of friends, the core of whom have remained my very best friends to this day. With them, I felt happy. I was as close to being myself as I ever was back then, and in the final couple of years at school, our social life really began to take off.

And yet, during the early years, as I walked through the school gates carrying my school bag over my shoulder, weighed down with folders and books, it would feel light in comparison to the weight of the insecurities I lugged around with me.

My self-image insecurities were never so evident as during my school days. I spent over an hour putting make-up on each morning in a bid to conceal my spotty face. The curtains would remain shut until I had my war paint on, in case anyone was passing and could see the real me. They'd run a mile.

They wouldn't run a mile.

Plus, I had absolutely no idea how to apply make-up back then, so the results were a fairly heavy-handed mask, with that tell-tale tidemark along the jawline.

Mum, very thoughtfully, even bought me a book on how to apply make-up. Not sure I replicated the pictures terribly well though, as the tidemark remained a feature.

And why is it that practically every girl opts for a shade of foundation ten times darker than their own skin tone when they first start to wear make-up? I did it too! My face was a deep orangey bronze colour, yet everything else from the neck down was white. Not a good look.

I spent what little money I had from my Saturday job in the local chemist on expensive hypoallergenic make-up, ever hopeful that it would magically heal my blemished skin. Needless to say, it didn't.

I'd have a daily battle against my unruly mop of wavy hair, desperate to flatten it down and straighten out the natural curl. How I longed for sleek, straight hair that would just blend in, and be unremarkable. My hair in its natural state attracted too much attention.

It attracted no attention at all.

And we mustn't overlook one key factor here. These were the days before proper hair straighteners hit the market. (The life-changing straighteners that were so powerful they could smooth out a poodle's coat!)

I was nothing if not a trier though, and went to great lengths to improvise in the meantime. I would arrange my head on the ironing board, lay my hair across it, and blindly aim the iron onto said locks. The end result was that I had horizontal burn marks from the iron on my neck, and my hair was more frizzy than ever before. All in all, not a complete success.

Again, the time I spent on the way I looked was not a tell-tale sign of teenage vanity. I wasn't titivating myself to make me stand out in the crowd. I was doing it so that I would be able to blend into the background.

The reality is that nobody was looking at me anyway. Why would they? I was just an average girl, no different from any of my classmates. Yes, I had bad spots, but so did several other poor souls. It's one of the many cruel afflictions to descend upon unfortunate teenagers.

Actually, I always thought it was worse for guys. They tended not to use make-up, so they didn't have any means of disguising their spots. Poor sods.

To this day my heart goes out to teenagers with bad skin. Any scarring from the spots themselves pales into insignificance compared to the mental scarring it can cause.

Yet although I'm sure nobody was paying any attention to me, my lack of confidence told me otherwise. I stood out, and for all the wrong reasons.

I'd sit at the back of the classroom wherever possible. This wasn't so that I could chat to my friends or get up to no good without the teacher noticing. It was so that nobody could sit behind me, therefore nobody could look at me.

School dances were a misery. There was a draconian system in place whereby all the girls would sit down one side of the school hall, and the boys sat down the other. Given their cue, the boys would then rush over and pick a girl to dance with.

So, the night of my first ever school dance arrived. It was 1986, and in keeping with the fashion of that era, I wore a beige, gathered mini skirt and a white shirt, tucked in, with an upturned collar for good measure. All the rage at the time, I promise! I'd used the diffuser on my hair, admitting defeat with my attempts to straighten it, so was sporting a full head of curls. The aim? To be mistaken for Kylie Minogue, (Charlene from *Neighbours*). The reality? To have nailed the look of a blonde Mick Hucknall. (Look him up if you really need to.)

After an initial period of milling around, waiting for the music to start and the dancing to begin, the teacher announced the first dance. A bit of a "rammy" ensued. The boys raced over (it was before they knew the merits of "playing it cool"), and one by one, amid much giggling and excitement, the row of girls whittled down as they were 'picked'. Gradually, all the couples took to the floor. The row of seats for the girls was empty. Or almost empty. There were three seats still in use, and three poor girls remained, trying their best to hide their humiliation and hurt. I know this, because I was one of them.

It turned out there were more girls than boys in our year, so this was always going to happen. But it was utterly hideous. I'll never forget having to watch all the other couples dance around the room, as us three "rejects" sat like muppets, trying our best to put on a brave face, while dying inside. I was actually fighting back tears. Once again, I stood out, but for the wrong reasons.

That whole experience haunted me for years to come, and worked wonders at deepening my feelings of insecurity and low self-esteem.

CHAPTER 4

UNREALISTIC EXPECTATIONS

'Why are you doing this to yourself, Alison? You're going to kill yourself.'

Mum was standing on the doorstep. It was snowing hard and she was only wearing her nightshirt and flimsy pink dressing gown.

The temperature had dropped to below zero, and I was being addressed by my Sunday name.

Mum was always very measured and never prone to exaggeration. She spoke simply and said it as it was. Any hints of sensationalism, or embellishing the facts for maximum impact, were unheard of, and yet here she was telling me I was going to kill myself.

As she stood on the doorstep, I could see she was fighting back tears. Again, unheard of. It's not that she was insensitive or lacking in emotion. Quite the reverse. But she always managed to put on a show of strength for the sake of my sisters and me. She was the cornerstone of our little family and would never have wanted to unsettle us by crying in front of us.

I'd only seen Mum cry once before, and that was after a dreadful family tragedy. So, this was bad.

I was 14 years old, and standing outside, wearing only my running shorts and sleeveless top. Plus, a baseball cap which was doing very little to protect me from the elements. That was mainly there to disguise me. Everyone would laugh if they saw me out running.

They wouldn't laugh.

A day or so earlier, the gremlin had announced with great conviction that I was the podgiest and ugliest girl in school. His case had been convincing. He had to be right.

I'd always been self-conscious. I'd always felt unattractive and stupid. But this was different. It had escalated into self-loathing. A disgust at the way I looked.

My voice was weird.

I was spotty.

My hair was horrible with its ugly waves and straw-like texture.

I looked ridiculous when I smiled.

I couldn't even walk properly. At least not like everyone else. I looked clumsy and, well, different.

All these negative beliefs felt horribly real to me in that moment. There was no question that they were a fabrication of my mind. They were fact.

They were not fact.

I was so sensitive that a couple of innocuous remarks here and there, from years back, had stuck.

There was one in particular, relating to the way I looked. I had bad acne which had started when I was about 11. That wasn't a figment of my imagination; it was real. I even went to the doctor about it and remember seeing her writing the words "angry acne" on my notes.

That did little to ease my discomfort!

I was given various lotions and washes to try to clear it up. I was even prescribed a contraceptive pill which was meant to get rid of acne. But nothing worked. Eventually, in my late teens, I was put on a strong medication called Roaccutane. It did the trick, but that was only after many years of trying to hide my gruesome face from the world. I would walk with my head tilted downwards and avoid eye contact when talking to people.

Roaccutane is a controversial medicine. They give it out far less readily now than they used to, but yours truly had two courses of it over the years. The most alarming side effect is its link to depression. The dermatologist who prescribed it for me knew my medical history, but must have felt it would pose no risks.

I'll never know whether it impacted on my mental state or not, but knowing what I know now, spots or no spots, I wouldn't go near it again. In fact, now that so much more is known about its side effects, I'm pretty certain it wouldn't be prescribed for me now, even if I wanted it. But back then, I really did want it ...

I was at the stables with Sue, who was the same age as me and very pretty. Quite how the subject came up, I don't know, but she announced that I either had chickenpox, or I didn't wash my face.

I just wanted to disappear. On the inside, I burst out crying, but I forced an unconvincing half-smile and a nod of agreement on the outside.

It was a cruel comment that would have upset anybody, but given my hypersensitivity, it crippled me. I desperately wanted to fit in but felt like an alien next to everyone else. It still upsets me now. I'm not upset for me. I'm upset for the little girl at the stables all those years ago. And for the teenage girl standing in the snow ...

'Why are you doing this to yourself, Alison? You're going to kill yourself.'

I felt as unattractive then as I had next to Sue. Yet, despite the unanimous decision in the case of "Ugly Ali versus the World", what the gremlin hadn't reckoned on was my strength of will. I would try to overturn the case, or at least win an appeal.

Cue the obsessive exercise and crash diet.

To put this into perspective, I was a perfectly healthy weight, and everything was perfectly in proportion. Well, everything apart from my ample chest. It was insanely generous and would have given Dolly Parton a run for her money. It was comedy gold! My boobs were like inflatable beach balls, but were in danger of turning into tennis balls in socks in the years to come.

The irony is that I was a late developer, and only a few years before then, I had been the proud owner of a 28AA padded bra, as I'd been the only girl in PE still wearing a vest!

A few years later, the offending, oversized appendages were surgically lopped off due to the back problems they were causing me, but for the time being, I was sporting a pretty impressive rack. I hated it. I hated myself.

Rack notwithstanding, I was suffering from a serious case of body dysmorphia, meaning that my perception of the way I looked was skewed. I saw flaws that simply weren't there. I was always comparing myself to others, but from an absurd point of view.

It wasn't a vanity thing. None of my hang-ups about the way I looked stemmed from me being vain. They were just another symptom of my troubled mental health.

My obsession at that time was to shrink to a size zero. Actually, I didn't know what a size zero was back then, but I knew I wanted to be teeny tiny. And I knew that, with a bit of hard graft, I'd soon look like the models in the glossy magazines.

That would surely make me happy. Wouldn't it? All my dark times would miraculously vanish. Wouldn't they?

Needless to say, I went about it in the most ridiculous and unhealthy way.

I began running almost as often as Forrest Gump, and reduced my calorie intake massively. Every morning, I'd get up at six o'clock and set off on my 4-mile round trip. I'd stop at the petrol station shop to buy a grapefruit for breakfast. Not the most obvious of places to buy your fresh fruit, but then I tended not to embrace the obvious.

I'd heard that eating a grapefruit burned calories. One of these little beauties a day would help me lose at least a stone. Or so I naïvely thought.

I went to school as normal, but as soon as I got home I'd change back into my running gear. After school, my run was a bit longer. It would take me to the local sports centre where I'd swim 40 lengths of the 25-metre pool.

Despite a determination that carried me through most things, even I was struggling with this demanding regime. I was sleepy at school and started getting headaches.

Unsurprisingly, this whole routine worried my poor mum enormously. I don't think it was the excessive exercise per se. There are worse obsessions. At least this one was based on health and fitness, unlike the obsessions that would come later in life. But for Mum, it was more linked to the fact that she was all too familiar with my obsessive ways, and was terrified about just how far I would take it.

That morning, as I stood shivering in the snow, it turned into an almighty stand-off. Mum's eyes welled up as she looked pleadingly at me, trying to coax me back inside.

She had no chance.

I've always been very sensitive. I can't bear to see anyone upset. Yet there I was breaking my mother's heart. I could have stopped Mum's tears so easily. All I had to do was walk back through the front door, change out of my completely inappropriate running gear into my school uniform, and sit down to breakfast with everyone else.

But I couldn't. I just couldn't. It was as if my emotional dial had got stuck in the off position. All this from the girl who would ordinarily have cut off a limb if it had meant stopping someone's tears. But in that moment, I was numb. My heart had frozen.

I felt no loving emotion, and in fact, was beginning to get angry about the fact something was getting in the way of my run. The fact it was my own mum didn't matter. I had to run. Immediately. It was all part of the plan, and for anything or anyone to disrupt that plan was simply not an option.

Later, I discovered that illnesses like bipolar can somehow take away your character and replace it with something that is quite the opposite of who you really are. And during those early years of living with my illness, I didn't recognise the person I would become. The Ali, as I'd always felt her to be, had vanished in place of the baddie in a James Bond film. Driven beyond belief, but without a heart. I didn't know it yet, but the little hints of bipolar behaviour were starting to stack up.

I was horribly confused, and I was beginning to question what was wrong with me. I felt sure there was something irregular about my thoughts and behaviour … I was certainly aware that my emotions seemed so much more extreme than those of anyone else around me. It was as though I felt more deeply, and was driven by compelling, visceral, fears.

I couldn't do anything about it though. Even if, on some level, I could feel myself careering towards a hypomanic or depressive episode, I still believed my thoughts to be rational and real. Afterwards though, I would always recognise that I'd lost my grip on reality for a little while.

There was always a dawning. It was as though my senses were being awakened and I was being re-booted to factory settings.

Back to Mum though, and it upsets me so much to think about the way I behaved that morning. My poor, poor mum.

I went for my run, bought my grapefruit, and later, put on my back pack for phase two at the swimming pool.

This obsessive phase lasted for about a month. I did lose weight. Weight that I didn't need to lose. But the breaking news is that it didn't stop the depression.

My self-esteem was still on the floor. My body shape was never going to improve my mental health.

After that month had passed, I just stopped. I stopped as suddenly as I had started. There was absolutely no reason for stopping, other than the fact that this particular obsession had passed to make way for whatever was going to temporarily spark my interest next.

It didn't take long for that next spark to ignite.

And unfortunately, my next obsession was making myself sick ...

I had come across some of Mum and Dad's old Carpenters records, and fell instantly in love with Karen Carpenter's beautiful voice. So pure, almost ethereal.

Then, by chance, I caught *The Karen Carpenter Story* on television one evening. Karen famously suffered with anorexia and bulimia nervosa, and the film depicted scenes where she would make herself sick.

To me, this seemed like a sensible next step in my quest to achieve happiness. Surely, if I could manage my weight in this way, it would bring me happiness in every aspect of my life. It would be an accomplishment to be able to feel in control of at least one facet of my being. I decided I would do it quietly, but felt sure that every time I was sick, it would take me one step closer to perfection.

Karen's long and agonising battle with anorexia had put so much stress on her heart over the years that she died from heart failure, aged just 32. It was desperately sad. It was also a pretty loud alarm bell, warning me just how damaging this cruel illness could be ...

I would be different though. I would be skinny and stay healthy.

With a bit of practice, I would become just as beautiful and strong as my new honey-voiced heroine.

Things didn't quite go to plan though. I wasn't very good at making myself sick. I'd leg it upstairs straight after dinner to lock myself away in the bathroom, where I'd shove my fingers down my throat. I'd twiddle them around my tonsils in an attempt to bring up Mum's offering of mince and potatoes. All this, while trying hard to muffle the noise of my retching. Invariably, I'd emerge a good 30 minutes later with a puffy face, bloodshot eyes, and a belly full of mince and potatoes.

That frustrated me no end. It angered me.

I did succeed on a few occasions and it felt absolutely amazing. Empowering. I loved the fact that none of what I'd eaten would have a chance to turn into fat, and that outwardly, I still appeared to be eating.

My Karen Carpenter obsession was all-consuming. I learnt the words to every single one of her songs. I watched the movie over and over again until I knew the entire script off by heart. I wouldn't just sing along to her songs, I would delve into the emotion of every word, to the point where I would cry sore tears.

I was grieving. I felt such sadness over a life which had been cut short so cruelly. But my emotions were disproportionate to the situation. It was almost as though I was forcing myself to endure grief and despair. Almost as though I wanted to be in that place.

My flirtation with an eating disorder was largely unsuccessful, and a phase that, thankfully, passed quickly.

Or so I thought. Really, it was more of a pause. A three-decade long pause.

CHAPTER 5

WHO AM I?

Throughout my teenage years, you could see the signs of emotional self-harm. I did my best to push my family away. All of them, but particularly my parents. I can vividly remember wanting to alienate myself. Wanting to be ignored and treated like an outcast. I wanted proof that I'd been right all along. That they didn't love me.

I even began to think I was adopted. How come I had blonde hair when no-one else did? Where had these enormous great knockers come from? How come I was so different in character from the rest of the family? This was more than just being the black (blonde) sheep, wasn't it?

I was living with four of the most placid, well-balanced and rational people you could ever hope to meet.

And then there was me.

The volatility was punctuated with periods of calm, during which I was a serious contender for the internationally recognised "Daughter of the Year" award. Kind, thoughtful, sweet and happy Ali would make a cameo appearance whenever she could.

Those appearances were limited though. Her angry, unkind, obsessive understudy would more often than not take centre stage. And the fight for the starring role was becoming more and more competitive.

There were countless shouting matches between Dad and I, two of which ended in me locking myself in the bathroom threatening to swallow an entire tub of paracetamol. As was so often the case, the shouting matches had stemmed from nothing of any great consequence, like negotiating what time I'd need to be home from my friend's house.

But, on each occasion, Dad had to break through the lock and retrieve me. I was a blubbering wreck, crying out for the love that had always been all around me, but that I couldn't see.

I was never going to take the paracetamol.

For years afterwards, both the bathrooms in the house had no lock. Risky business going to the toilet in our house!

There were times when my rage was so far out of control that I was almost in a trance-like state. I wouldn't just get irate; I would become someone that neither I, nor my family, recognised. And the change of mood was as quick as it was devastating.

Everyone can become frustrated or angry, but later I found out that this absolute loss of control is one of the main symptoms of bipolar rage.

I'd really ramp up the ante with Dad. I'd desperately try to come up with the most hateful and cruel things to say, and scream nastiness at him, with as much venom as I could muster.

I'd show him that I'd been right all along: that I was adopted, and they didn't love me. In the end, he'd have to admit that they'd always regretted bringing me into their otherwise perfect family. I'd catch him out sooner or later.

Dad was adopted, and I think that's what planted the seed within me that I too was adopted.

During these horribly ugly fights, I'd scream obscenities at him, which for my respectful, churchgoing parents was deeply upsetting.

One of the worst things I said is almost too excruciating to repeat. I called Dad something that hurt him to the core.

Even though I was ill, I was racked with guilt afterwards. But the damage had already been done.

In my mind, I had always been victimised by my parents who hated the sight of their evil, adopted daughter. So, I spat the words out. I screamed them. I just wanted to hurt him.

I called my gentle, kind dad a bastard.

I can picture his face now. It was a look of shock, but more than anything, a look of great sadness. His beloved, yet deeply troubled, daughter had hurt him more than he'd ever been hurt by anyone else in his life.

Immediately after saying it, I knew I had gone too far. The guilt, quite rightly, quietened my rage and I wanted to take it all back.

Guilt affects everyone in different ways. Not surprisingly, given my extreme reactions to everything in life, it was so emotionally corrosive for me that it would send me into a spiral of deep depression. I deserved that though. And I realise I'm putting myself out there by sharing this. I want to be honest though. I want to talk about what happened truthfully. To demonstrate the extent to which my illness took over and turned me into the polar opposite of what I was at heart.

The thing is, I loved my dad (and my mum) more than anyone else in the world. And more than anything, I wanted them to love me.

They did. What I got was nothing less than unconditional love. The depth of their love was unquestionable, but my mind had convinced me otherwise, so a defiant self-protection mechanism kicked in. If they didn't love me, I had to protect myself from that hurt. I'd have to give as good as I got ...

It must have been awful for my family to live with such erratic behaviour. The outbursts of anger, the recklessness and the desperation to hurt them as much as I could. How hard must it have been for my parents not to take it personally? Not to react to it? My sisters were (and are) both so emotionally balanced;

living with my disruptive and hateful behaviour must have hacked them off too.

I couldn't have blamed them if it did. But if I couldn't understand what was going on, how on earth could they?

On the face of it, I was an angry, moody, selfish teenager with no regard for the way I upset those closest to me.

I know now that I was ill. That none of that was really me. And so do my family. It still happened though, and it was devastating for all of us.

CHAPTER 6

A DANGER TO SOCIETY?

As I progressed through school, another twist to my character revealed itself. I was nearing the stage of deciding what to do with my life after I left school, and was veering towards a career choice which would seem entirely at odds with my awkward, shy personality.

I became dead-set on becoming a television presenter.

This from the girl who got self-conscious walking into the classroom!

But I had a theory that if I became a TV presenter, I would automatically become cool, calm and composed. People would look at me and think, *she's got it all.*

I would be *that girl.* The girl with no anxieties or insecurities, just a warm, easy demeanour, and a perfect home life. I would command everyone's respect.

Oh, and obviously I would be spot-free and have shiny, straight hair too.

The only slight fly in the ointment was that Mum and Dad were keen for me to go to university. I'm sure that they, like most people, felt that making a career in TV was a bit of a pipe dream, so they wanted me to have something "to fall back on."

But I had made up my mind that I was TV-bound and had no interest whatsoever in any of the university courses on offer.

I flicked through the prospectuses one evening anyway, to keep Mum and Dad happy, and randomly picked out a three-year degree course in Business and Marketing. It sounded equally as dull as the rest of the courses on offer, but would appease my parents and give me time to plan my career as "Broadcaster of the Year".

The good news was that my transition from school to university was non-eventful. The bad news was that I simply transferred my insecurities and low self-esteem from one learning establishment to another. Or so I thought ...

Funnily enough though, despite having no interest in the course I was doing, it did serve a purpose. I slowly began to come out of my shell. At least, a little bit. I still had the inferiority complex of an anxious child desperate to live up to expectations. (Expectations imposed on me by myself.) But there was a gradual shift from being a constantly pained young woman, to someone who was ever so slightly growing into her own skin.

I didn't rush to sit at the back of the lecture theatre. I would even volunteer some answers and participate in the seminars.

My personality hadn't dramatically changed. I was still intrinsically insecure, but was getting better at fighting the urges to want to disappear.

Throughout my three years at university, I continued to experience my now predictably wild fluctuations in mood. The highs tended to play out on social occasions, when I would seek to be the most outrageous or the funniest person there. Looking back on it now, I can't tell you how humiliated this makes me feel. The lows could descend at any point, but particularly during intense periods of study.

My OCD tendencies prevailed, and mainly manifested through excessive cleaning and tidying. And that included me personally. I showered at least twice a day and brushed and flossed my teeth at least three times a day.

I was a wear-once-then-wash kind of a girl too. Even if I was wearing something dark-coloured, I'd worry that the grubbiness of the day, although it wouldn't have been visible, would still be there. If it weren't for the fact that everything would have shrunk, I'd have put my clothes in a boil wash every time to make sure they were totally clean.

I'd completely remove my make-up, multiple times a day if possible, so that I could thoroughly cleanse my face, and then re-apply it.

It was an exhausting way to live.

As for my issue with body dysmorphia, it made a dramatic U-turn. Rather than filling my spare time with marathon runs and grapefruits, I began to fill my stomach with donuts and crisps. Over a period of just a few months, I piled on an impressive stone in weight.

But once again, my perception of reality was skewed. Whereas I used to see myself as being much larger than I actually was, I actually couldn't recognise the extent to which I had ballooned. And I would lurch from eating an insane amount to practically starving myself. I was locked into doing everything to extremes.

The fluctuations in my weight back then were reflective of my existence. There was no consistency.

Away from university, my social life was good though. I made friends during my studies, but mainly socialised with my school buddies. We'd go out every weekend, pubbing and clubbing. Despite never feeling good about the way that I looked, I still loved our social antics.

We were always full of mischief, but didn't fall into the category of being "bad girls". Our antics were still acceptable fodder to tell our parents. Like the time we were in a cab coming back from a night out. For some reason, we thought the cab driver was taking an unnecessarily long route home. It's just possible that our perception of our "close to the edge but charming humour" was a little blurred due to the amount of peach schnapps we'd daintily downed, and the cab driver, probably quite reasonably, pulled over and ordered us all out of his car!

Unfazed, we zigzagged our way towards one of the girls' houses, congratulating ourselves on our hilarious wit, then all of a sudden became aware of a car driving slowly towards us from behind. We couldn't see it as we had just navigated a corner in the road, but assumed it was the bemused cab driver coming back to collect his fare, which he'd seemingly overlooked, much to our glee.

Giggling and shrieking like banshees, we all legged it into a nearby garden and hid behind various bushes and trees. As the noise of the engine grew closer, we remained in our ill-thought-out hiding places, waiting for the car to pass.

It didn't pass though. In fact, it pulled up right in front of the garden we were in. Our giggles subsided a little then, in place of nervous laughter. This was all a bit creepy.

The next thing we heard was a stern voice. 'Come out of the garden now. We know you're there.' The flashing blue lights of the police car then came into focus as we slowly emerged from behind the undergrowth.

Now at that point, we weren't to know whether the police were going to arrest us, or worse still, take us home to our parents. Nonetheless, as we sheepishly walked towards the two policemen, I decided the most sensible course of action was to throw my arms up in the air and declare that we were unarmed!

This made the rest of the girls howl. Once again, we were laughing uproariously, but thankfully had the good grace to continue our stagger towards the boys in blue.

Luckily, the policemen had sussed out that we were neither a danger to society, nor the burglars they had first suspected when they had pulled up.

They didn't share the same degree of amusement about our escapades as we did, but very decently, just told us to get home safely and keep out of any more gardens on the way.

We dutifully agreed. But just as we turned to go, one of the girls thought to ask how they had known we were in the garden in the first place.

Turns out we'd triggered the security lights, flooding the entire garden with light. Not one of us had even noticed.

That peach schnapps was good stuff.

CHAPTER 7

DRIVING MY PARENTS UP THE WALL

By my late teens, my mood swings didn't so much resemble a clock pendulum as a steel wrecking ball. They swung heavily from one direction to the other, and caused just as much damage as a wrecking ball on a tower block.

The main difference was that whereas the wrecking ball would move in a regular motion, my moods were as irregular as arrhythmia. The gremlin had become stronger than me. He tormented the hell out of me whenever he felt like it.

Turning 17 was a milestone for me, as it is for many teenagers in the UK, and it meant only one thing …

Driving lessons!

I could just see it. In no time at all, I'd be emulating the girls who had already turned 17. I'd be the one jangling the car keys when we went out, saying in a stage whisper, 'Just a coke for me, thanks. I'm driving.'

I had it all planned. I'd work every hour under the sun. £8.25 per hour for my job as an usherette at the theatre should do it – and I'd still make it in for the odd lecture at university. (We start uni early in Scotland.) In no time at all, I'd be the proud owner of my very own wheels.

I'd wear shades for every single journey, whatever the weather. My car would be black and shiny. The seat belt would have a faint whiff of the very expensive perfume I would somehow have acquired, and under no circumstances would I ever crash.

So. Driving lesson number one.

As I'd feared, the instructor's car was decidedly un-black and shiny. It was an ancient, beaten-up old hatchback. And it did smell, but not of expensive perfume. It had a rather unpleasant stale, damp smell.

That was all okay though. This was just a means to an end.

Off we went to the little housing estate where I was to be let loose on the roads for the first time.

Engine on. Car in gear. Mirrors, signal, manoeuvre. I was off.

I continued with my weekly lessons, but also went out with Dad as often as possible. But, oh dear. That was never going to go well.

I didn't like to be wrong. Predictably though, I was wrong quite a lot during my lessons with Dad. There were numerous heated exchanges.

'I was just about to do that!'

'I *was* braking, you just didn't notice.'

'I know they're the windscreen wipers, but that's where the indicators are on the instructor's car.'

On my final outing with Dad, I pulled over, demonstrating the perfect emergency stop, leapt out of the car, slammed the door shut, and stormed off, screaming that he should drive if he was so bloody perfect.

Possibly not the best attitude towards someone who was trying to help me, but entirely consistent with my angry behaviour towards my poor dad. And that was the end of my extra lessons with Dad.

My test date arrived a few months later. The clutch broke during my test which did nothing for my inner calm.

But miraculously, I coped, and passed first time. It meant I was free to jangle those keys, wear my shades, day and night, and fill my car with the beautiful aroma of my non-existent expensive perfume.

Ah yes, my car ... My £8.25 per hour hadn't yet stretched to securing me my own car, but Mum and Dad were very good at letting me take the family car. Not that I deserved it with the way I treated them.

It was a bright red Volvo 240. It was longer than your average intercity train, and a far cry from the teeny little car I had been used to driving during my lessons. It was known in the family as "the tank". I was delighted though, and grateful to my parents for the use of their car. But, on the day I passed my test, I switched from being a good, if somewhat inexperienced, driver to being a danger on the roads.

I look back and shudder.

As soon as I got behind the wheel I was Lewis Hamilton, in pole position to scoop the Formula 1 Championship. I can remember feeling the adrenaline course through my body before I'd even fastened my seatbelt.

At times, it could just take the shortest of car journeys to trigger a hypomanic episode which might go on for the rest of the day or more.

I felt uncontrollably excited. My confidence was through the roof. The sunroof that is. I was the best driver ever to have graced the roads. I was invincible ... but I was also impatient. I was often angry. I was easily distracted. And I was aggressive. I took risks. Big risks.

Once again, I would become someone I didn't recognise. There were times when, quite simply, I was an irresponsible young driver. That was bad enough. But it was the hypomanic episodes that posed the biggest danger.

I crashed the car twice in the space of two months. Thankfully, no one was hurt on either occasion.

The first accident happened when I was on the way to collect a friend. There was a birthday meal in town for one of my university friends, and I was chief key jangler. It was a miserable winter's evening. It was dark. The rain was bouncing off the ground. It was windy. I was late.

I was speeding along far too fast, and as I approached a bend in the road I slammed on the brakes. I fully expected the car to hug the corner, when once again I'd press the accelerator to the floor, before congratulating myself on my driving prowess.

That's not what happened.

As soon as I hit the brakes, the car careered across the narrow road and spun, before crashing through a garden wall.

At that point, you might think I'd have snapped out of my idiocy and realised I wasn't the invincible champion driver I believed myself to be.

Instead, I can clearly remember taking all of five seconds to regroup. I reversed the tank out of the garden wall, slid back into first gear, and continued on my journey.

It defies belief. But I was in such a state of hypomania that nothing had any true meaning. I felt no fear. No remorse at having vandalised some poor soul's wall. No guilt. And no care for the fact I could so easily have hurt someone. Or worse.

Having picked up my friend and driven to the restaurant, we had a quick look at the car. The front left wing was badly damaged. Not to worry though. We had a birthday to celebrate.

Still high as a kite, I dominated conversation throughout the evening. I laughed the loudest. I reacted more than anyone else at the stories being told. I was an embarrassment. This behaviour, you'll remember, was not alcohol-related.

At the end of the evening, I dropped my friend back home before getting myself and the tank back to my parents' house. I sped up the short driveway before screaming to a standstill inches before hitting the garage door.

Good. A successful night.

The following morning, I woke early. The hypomania had been replaced by a horrible low. I felt heavy, tearful and empty. Most of all though, there was that all-too-familiar feeling of desperate sadness.

As was always the case following a hypomanic episode, it felt a bit like a dream. Or a nightmare. It was a bit like looking back on a drunken night, and waiting for all the pieces to fit back together.

I crept into Mum and Dad's bedroom as soon as I heard Radio 4 start up on their radio alarm.

Mum asked how my night had been …

Now the right thing to do would have been to own up to having been a complete idiot, explain what had happened, and assure them I had learnt my lesson.

The wrong thing to do would have been to tell them that someone must have crashed into the car while I was in the restaurant having dinner with my friends.

I opted for explanation number two.

This part of the story has now become family folklore. I am the worst liar known to man.

Dad went out to inspect the car in his dressing gown, while I waited for him to come in muttering about how inconsiderate and dishonest other drivers could be. I would, of course, agree heartily.

Instead, he came in with a puzzled look on his face. A puzzled, yet knowing, look. And he looked stern.

'So, there was no damage to the car before you parked?'

'No.'

'You're sure?'

'Yep.'

Still waiting for the muttering of discontent about other drivers.

'Hm. I'm just confused as to how there would be moss wedged into the damaged wing. Almost like moss that would grow on a wall.'

He was good.

'I guess the other car must have had moss on it?'

My explanation didn't wash.

Dad 1 – Ali 0.

I was made to go and speak to the owners of the wall and ensure that it was put right. That was the least I could do.

So surely, I mean surely, I'd have learnt my lesson by then. Not so. As soon as the repaired tank came out of the body shop, I crashed it again.

This crash was slightly different. The type of damage to the car was the same, only this time, it was on the opposite wing.

I was banned from driving the car until I took an advanced driving lesson. My poor parents. Again. There was just a constant stream of trouble from the middle daughter.

At that point though, my approach to driving changed. The reality of what could have happened during my spell of F1 driving finally hit home. The car, thankfully, hit neither the home, nor any more walls.

CHAPTER 8

HEDONISTIC HEIGHTS

I was no paragon of virtue. In fact, from my teenage years, right through to the time my illness was diagnosed at the age of 35, I was, at times, completely off the rails.

I was guilty of binge drinking. Regularly.

Towards the end of my time at university, I began dabbling with recreational drugs. In waves.

The drugs started with speed and ecstasy, before I moved onto cocaine.

The binge drinking started at around the same time. I didn't know what was going on in my head then, and I wasn't on any meds, but I'm afraid to say that it continued later, when I was on antidepressants in my late teens and twenties. (Okay, and my early thirties.) Not clever. I may not have had a diagnosis, but I was mentally ill, and illegal substances were never going to bring me stability.

There came a point much further down the line when I had to accept I had a problem with drink. Before that though, I managed to squeeze in some dreadful behaviour. I drank to forget. To lose my inhibitions. To be funny and outrageous. I nailed the outrageous part, but would question how funny I actually was.

I'm sure the effects of alcohol were heightened when I did end up being on meds, but I didn't care. The self-destruct button was well and truly switched on, and remained lit up for many years to come.

I had no self-worth whatsoever, and as a result, my judgement was severely lacking. Inappropriate relationships featured heavily. I was no longer that sorrowful little girl who didn't get picked at the school dance. I'd date a guy for a couple of weeks, fall desperately in love, then move on to someone else. I could just about manage to remember their name during their two-week window.

There are names for girls like me. Or at least girls like I used to be.

There is nothing about this period in my life about which I feel proud. I was stupid and rash. I was cruel and selfish. I hurt people. I absolutely hate admitting to that, but I have to because it's true. I hurt people.

As for the drugs, and as for what on earth was I thinking – that's a very simple question for me to answer. I just didn't care. I didn't care about me. What did I matter?

I always cared deeply for my friends and family, despite the way I treated the latter, but never came close to affording myself even the teeniest part of that care.

My friends and I would head into Glasgow on a Saturday night, and irrespective of the way the girls conducted themselves, I would drink my weight in alcohol. Bearing in mind I'm only 5ft 3in, my alcohol consumption was way out of proportion for my size.

After the pub we'd the head to a nightclub. Once again, I'd choose to ignore the conduct of my friends and take ecstasy or speed.

That world of intoxicants had opened up to me at university ...

I'd got chatting to a guy in a bar one night, who happened to be looking for a singer. He was a prolific and talented songwriter, and wrote jazzy/funky stuff with a bit of a Prince (or "squiggle") vibe. A few days later I auditioned for him, and he must have liked what he heard as he asked me to front his band. I was chuffed to bits! I loved the thought that we'd be touring the world, playing in stadiums to hundreds of thousands of adoring fans.

I'd nip off to rehearsals between lectures, and loved the feeling of being amongst such a talented bunch of musicians. I felt free. Joyful. Uninhibited. And even, dare I say it, worthy of my place in the line-up.

It was almost as though I adopted a new and liberated persona as soon as I stepped into the rehearsal room or the studio. I'd drop the heavy burdens of anxiety and angst, and instead, pick up a weightless, carefree sense of freedom.

The social life with the band was lively, to say the least. On one occasion when we were all out, someone produced a wrap of speed and offered it to me. I was nervous. Unfortunately, though, and possibly quite predictably, my overriding emotion was one of excitement. And curiosity. I wanted to try everything. I was a thrill seeker.

After trying it that first time, and enjoying the rush, taking it again when I went clubbing didn't seem like such a big deal. But putting that stuff into my body was playing havoc with my mental wellbeing.

Everything I did, let's not forget, I did to extremes.

The rush of inflated ego when I was clubbing, the extreme joy, and the desire to talk to people (very quickly) made me feel happy. I lost my inhibitions. I would dance all night.

I would also overheat, which apart from being dangerous, must have been a fairly unattractive look. I'd scrape my hair back into a messy bun and dance like nobody was watching. I do so hope they weren't watching.

Any thoughts of what the drugs were doing to my heart were pushed aside for that temporary feeling of euphoria.

When I look back, I'm dumbfounded. It defies belief. How short-sighted. How stupid.

As for the effects on my mood afterwards? The lows which sometimes followed paled into insignificance compared to the deep depressions I had suffered long before I'd ever started using drugs. So, it seemed worth taking the hit over the next couple of days, just to experience the joy of that moment.

In my warped mind, I wasn't doing anyone any harm, except myself. And that mattered not a jot.

Alcohol went on to become a big problem. Whereas it had been the preserve of nights out in the early days, it escalated into a more frequent abuse.

In the years to come, I would drink on my own most evenings. Wine and champagne. My flat was always well-stocked with both, but the supplies had to be replenished frequently.

I'd buy in bulk at the supermarket, and invariably heard myself explaining to the cashier that I was having a party. To actually feel embarrassed about the amount of alcohol I was buying should have told me something.

But it didn't.

CHAPTER 9

BREAKDOWN

I was 19. I had just graduated from university with a BA in Business Studies.

I know that seems very young to have come through university, but it was just a combination of the Scottish school system and the way my birthday fell. I was no child prodigy.

And, bold as I was all those years ago, I didn't invest in a briefcase. I had my eye on a microphone. I still wanted to be a television presenter.

I hadn't left home yet, so made the most of the board and lodgings at my parents' house, while trying to break into the notoriously difficult world of television.

I continued with my job in the theatre so that I was earning a bit of money while trying to nail down a career. I also took on a second job working behind a bar in a cool little pub. I was absolutely shocking at this. I'm a complete klutz and spilt more pints than I served.

I settled down for a bit, and replaced my hard partying with industriousness and conscientious activity. It was a busy time, but I was so determined to give TV my best shot that I juggled my jobs and became a one-woman enterprise. This was a serious business, and my obsessive side turned out to be a great asset.

The head office of 'Operation TV' was in my parents' box room. The computer was a hand-me-down Commodore 64, complete with 5¼" floppy discs. The previous owner had upgraded to a ZX Spectrum!

There were timetables. There were working hours. There were immaculately kept files detailing which producers I had contacted and when to chase them up. There was a constant stream of trade journals, like The Stage and TV, landing on the doormat for me to scour in search of my dream job. There were books on how to become a TV presenter.

I worked solidly at breaking down doors. More often than not, those doors were slammed shut in my face, but I just kept trying.

Then, a year into my search, something snapped ...

I had been trying to get work in what everyone knew, and most of them were telling me, was one of the toughest industries to break into. And I had been dealing with one knock back after another. Even with my track record of pushing myself to the point of exhaustion, my strength had evaporated. I was tired of faking a smile.

I was utterly exhausted. Exhausted by pretending to be well. My smile had turned into tears. I couldn't go on trying any longer. And that's when I had my first nervous breakdown.

At the time of writing, that was 24 years ago, but it still feels as real today as it did back then.

It probably shouldn't have come as any great surprise. I had always come across as being strong, determined and happy, but without really knowing it, I'd been battling mental illness since I was a little girl.

In the weeks leading up to my breakdown, my mood had taken a massive dip. My motivation had waned. I'd stopped wanting to contact people. I barely spoke to anyone in either of my two jobs. Physically I was there, but mentally I was miles away.

A few people asked if I was okay ... if I'd broken my leg, I would have told them that it hurt. But because I was depressed, I just said that I felt a bit tired, but otherwise, I was feeling absolutely fine.

I lost a fair bit of weight. It wasn't a conscious decision; it wasn't my anorexia at work. It was another symptom of having no interest in anything. Including food.

It all came to a head one evening when I got home from the theatre. I just broke down. All the tears that hadn't been allowed to fall over the preceding weeks and months came out that night. I cried until my eyes were red and swollen.

I needed my mum, and she held me tightly. She quietly reassured me; she told me that I was just utterly exhausted. That I had run myself into the ground.

She was right.

But of course, there was more to it than that. We still didn't know the whole story. We didn't know I was living with an undiagnosed mental illness. Looking back, I don't know how on earth I'd got through life that far.

The emotional pain was excruciating. I was in turmoil. Chaos ran riot in my bewildered young mind. I was seriously depressed. I was confused. I was lost.

More than anything though, I was exhausted.

The pressure of holding everything together, while careering through the past year at a speed that would have impressed a cheetah, had inevitably taken its toll.

Mum and Dad were incredible. Dad had always tended to be the decision maker. It's not that he dominated in any way. I just think that dynamic suited them. It worked.

But when daughter number two has a nervous breakdown?

Wow. Mum should really have started wearing her pants over her trousers to fit her superhero status. Like Julie Andrews in The Sound of Music, Mum rallied during the storm. Her immeasurable strength came into its own.

Surprisingly, I slept soundly that night. I didn't move until the following morning, when Mum came upstairs with a coffee and an action plan.

I was still reeling. My head was spinning. It was all happening in slow motion though, like a spinning top that was about to topple over.

Mum exuded a calm but dynamic air. She was in mother hen mode and was clucking so loudly that chicks were flocking to the front door. She propped up my pillows in the way she must have done for her patients when she'd been a nurse, and handed me my coffee. She held my hand and stroked it with her thumb, then told me that she'd made an emergency appointment with the GP at 10.30am. I was numb. I'd have attended an emergency appointment with a bucket full of frogs, if that's what had been organised for me.

The GP took my breakdown seriously. She was a kind lady and asked insightful questions. I'm not sure the same could be said about my answers.

She asked about what I was doing workwise. I told her.

Had anything in particular triggered this low? I didn't know.

Had I had any ideations of suicide? Fleetingly.

I was way too far gone to have any real clarity. But I do remember her observation that I was dressed all in black. I often dressed in black and had never thought about it. The doctor suggested it was a reflection of my mood and that perhaps I should wear something with a bit more colour.

I never did follow that piece of advice. Black will always be my fashion go-to. And I don't believe that depression necessarily follows obvious stereotypes. Not everyone who dresses in black, listens to Nirvana or cries 24/7.

The next thing I knew, I was sitting in the car waiting for Mum to come back from the pharmacy. The upshot of my visit to the doctor had been that I was suffering with depression and anxiety. Despite my numbed state, that shocked me.

Depression is an actual illness. Other poor souls suffered with depression. But me? Not me, surely …

Mum returned to the car with a little paper bag containing a box of Prozac. I was horrified at the prospect of being on antidepressants.

I needn't have been afraid, but I couldn't help it. What did life with depression mean? Was I going to feel like this for the rest of my life?

In the days and weeks to come I stayed under the radar. Mum had called both the theatre and the pub to say that I was ill and would be taking some time off. This from the woman who would have sent us to school, even if we'd lost a leg. We did have another leg after all.

I had given Mum a real fright. She was shocked at seeing her daughter suffer such a major breakdown. Any reservations she would normally have had about letting work down were cast aside. Her daughter was ill. Extremely ill.

I was 19 years old, and incapable of functioning.

The Prozac didn't kick in for several weeks, so my only medication in the meantime was rest. I needed to mentally switch off, something I had always found extremely difficult to do. My total loss of energy did at least make that feel a little easier.

I spent a lot of time sleeping. I lay in bed until midday most days, and when I did eventually did get up, I'd make my way along the corridor from my bedroom, down the stairs, through the kitchen, and onto the sofa. That was just about all I could face.

I did a world of sobbing. I'd lie on the sofa staring at absolutely nothing, wondering how on earth I'd ended up in this situation. I felt dead inside.

Mum is always super-busy, but she did some nifty diary juggling to cancel or postpone as much as she could, so that she could be with me.

We didn't talk much. We sat together a lot, which I liked, and at times, Mum would ask what I was feeling. She was desperate to understand, so that she could try to help me, but didn't want to put me under any pressure.

I had no words anyway.

It wasn't that I didn't want to open up. I did. I desperately wanted to be able to put into words what I was feeling, but I just couldn't. I had no feelings. It was as though my brain was jammed; as if it needed to be taken to bits and put back together again. But I had no idea how to do that. What did I need to do to re-join the world?

When I was curled up on the sofa on my own, I would listen as Mum bustled about in the kitchen. When it got to about 4.30pm, she'd ask the dog the rhetorical question of whether she'd like her dinner. (The dog always replied yes, incidentally.)

She'd empty the washing machine and hang up the wet clothes on the pulley. She'd sweep the kitchen floor.

Hearing that everyday soundtrack being played out in those first couple of weeks was of such enormous comfort. It took me back to when I was a child, and I was off school with a tummy bug. I felt safe. I could hide away from reality, cocooned in this cotton wool environment.

It's funny though. When I had been working, there were so many times that I wished I could just chill out for a while and watch back-to-back, black-and-white movies. But this deep depression stole any desire even to watch television. I had the concentration of a gnat, so staring into nothing was the best I could manage.

I must have spent at least two weeks in that state, but as time went on, my soul began to wake up. It was a very slow and inconsistent process – one step forward, two steps back. Crucially though, there was progress. I was gathering strength to live again.

As my strength built, I would occasionally join Mum as she walked the dog on the moor. It was a risky business though.

Meeting anyone I knew carried the threat of needing to interact. Talking? That was way out of the question. What I really needed was for her to be my motorcycle outrider, clearing the path ahead for me to walk through uninterrupted.

Like phase one though, this too passed. I gravitated to sitting on the kitchen worktop chatting with Mum, rather than lying in a vegetative state on the sofa.

Then, what would have been unthinkable a few weeks beforehand, became manageable. I'd join Mum when she went to the supermarket, where we'd invariably meet someone we knew, and chat. Not for long, but it was a start.

The Prozac wasn't a miracle cure for the misery that the breakdown had created, but it did … I think … help me to reach a place where I could begin to help myself.

It took a good six weeks for the worst of the deep depression to pass, but as the days and weeks rolled by, my mood gradually lifted, and I re-joined society.

I never did go back to work at the pub, but I went back to the theatre, and picked up where I'd left off with my job search. So, in the space of those six weeks, I had gone full circle, and arrived back at 'Operation TV'.

It had been a slow transition from my depressive episode to the hypomanic stage this time, as though the gremlin wanted me to endure every single negative emotion before moving me onto a high. But I was soon running at full pelt once again.

My breakdown certainly didn't give me a lesson in slowing down. If anything, it made me want to make up for lost time; somehow, I found another gear.

What had I been thinking about, lounging around on the sofa for all those weeks? What if the job I had been searching for had come up during that time, and I had been too busy staring to sniff it out?

I was in a state of panic.

I'd ignore my own schedule and put in hours of "unpaid overtime". I'd squeeze in all the shifts I possibly could at the theatre. In the process, I all but cut off my friends, for fear that they would distract me from my mission.

I was on the fast train to my dream job and there was no scheduled stop until it reached its final destination.

The job eventually materialised.

At the age of 20, I landed the role of presenter of a teenage magazine show on Scottish TV, secretly carrying my diagnosis of depression and anxiety with me.

I was about to begin a two decades' long career as a television presenter, and it was just as well I didn't know what lay ahead for me. Because what was to unfold would take me to the lowest point in my life to date.

CHAPTER 10

ALL-TIME LOW

My rise up the career ladder was swift.

I spent three and a half years co-presenting the teenage magazine show. It was an absolute blast!

One week I'd be presenting a report from a zoo with a 6ft long python draped around my neck (not so lovely), and the next I'd be interviewing Boyzone (I really fancied Ronan Keating, the lead singer). I got to interview him twice, and the second time, I was in the middle of introducing myself, and he interrupted me, piping up in his dreamy Irish accent, 'I've met you before!'

Can you even begin to imagine for one single nanosecond what that did to me?!

Now. Had I been cool, I'd have nodded and smiled, and perhaps reminded him where it was I'd last interviewed him. But no. I did that whole goofy thing of mumbling about the first time we'd met, while going bright red, and looking at the ground as I fidgeted off-puttingly with the zip on my jacket. Thankfully, I had a stern word with myself, and we ended up having a fantastic interview. I found my voice, and completely settled down.

We had a real laugh in fact, only at one point, the laugh was on me.

I wanted to know how the boys chilled out after the buzz of having just performed on stage to thousands of adoring fans, and they kept going on about how "Jack" helped them to relax. Eventually I asked them who this Jack was, and they all fell about laughing.

It turns out they were referring to the drink, Jack Daniels, and how quaffing a couple of Jacks after performing was the best way to wind down.

That little anecdote actually ended up in the paper the next day. *Ali's TV blunder*.

I didn't mind though – it was all in good humour. And I was still in seventh heaven after having spent a few hours with the legend that was Ronan Keating.

While I was presenting the magazine show, I was asked to guest present on a holiday programme. Then I went on to present a live political debate show. There was an animal show; a live, Sunday morning, current affairs show; and a few more programmes besides.

On the face of it, life was good.

I was making a living doing my dream job, and my career looked to be on the up and up.

When I was 23, I bought my first flat and my first car. The car, incidentally, was neither black nor shiny, and thankfully, I'd realised by then that wearing my shades on every journey may just have made me look like a bit of a fool.

But, by then I was drinking heavily and taking cocaine from time to time. Never when I was working though. I'd worked hard to create my career and had too much respect for the job. It was when the studio door closed behind me at the end of the day that I'd give in to my demons.

Plus of course, there were still plenty of mood swings. My emotional weighing scales were out of control. They would tip at any given moment. The hypomanic episodes were far more frequent than ever before, and were always followed by the inevitable ghastly lows.

Even when I was on set in the studio I'd experience hypomania. I couldn't get my words out quickly enough. I was desperate to hear everything my interviewees had to say. I hung on their every word, which must have made my interviews a weird and intense experience for them. But to me it seemed that, whatever the subject, it was the most fascinating topic in the world.

I'd be bursting with energy when I delivered my words to camera. I'd research every little detail of whatever it was we were covering in the show. It wasn't just normal preparation though, it was obsessive research which turned me into a professor of each subject. I think I became more of an expert in those subjects than our expert guests were.

I was attracting a fair bit of media attention. I sensed that I was admired and respected, but I couldn't accept that I was worthy of it.

There were countless features about me in the newspapers, mainly focused on my work, but sometimes on my private life. I hated that, but I don't believe anyone in the public eye can complain too much about mild intrusion. Yes, they do very often overstep the bounds of decency and respect, but without that publicity, you wouldn't be in demand.

It was getting to the point where I would sometimes be stopped in the street and asked for an autograph. Strangers would talk to me as if they knew me.

And yet, I felt terribly alone.

To the outside world, I had it all. I knew that I was lucky. I knew that I was blessed in so many ways, but the inside story was often very different.

I spent my first nine years in the business in constant work. It felt like I was always on TV. But then, the harsh reality hit me. Almost as suddenly as my career had taken off, the work all but dried up.

As far as I could see, there was no specific reason for it. I hadn't become a bad presenter overnight.

I knew the life of a TV presenter could be horribly unpredictable. To sustain yourself through one short period of lean times is pretty good going, but of course at the time, there was no knowing just how long that fallow period would last.

In the end, it lasted about six months, and it was tough. Given that I had a mortgage and bills to pay, that was long enough to put me under financial strain.

On top of that, I was still living with an undiagnosed illness. And every now and then, the volcano inside me would erupt, and do its usual indiscriminate damage to my life.

I tried hard to keep my spirits up. I read self-help books. I even read the Bible. I went running every day.

I spent more time on my appearance. My nails were immaculately manicured. I wore make-up every day. I straightened my hair (the life-changing straighteners were around by then – no more ironing), and even treated it to a regular hair mask.

Thanks to my obsessive side, my flat was permanently in show-home mode. But none of that was going to help keep a roof over my head.

The drugs were off the menu, but the drink was still an issue. Something had to change.

I had an inspired idea. I decided to sign up with a temping agency and see whether anyone would give me a job as a personal assistant to some high-flying businessman.

I had no shorthand skills and I had never filed anything other than my own TV papers. And, in truth, I wasn't entirely sure what the role of a PA entailed, but I gladly bought into the cliché about the glamorous jet-set lifestyle.

I duly signed up with an agency and was soon contacted with a temporary job offer. Exciting! Soon I'd be flying around the world in the boss's private jet, taking notes while he dictated to me, and organising an anniversary present for his wife.

It didn't quite work out that way for me.

The job in question was a receptionist in a scaffolding company. It was run from a glorified portacabin in an industrial estate in one of the roughest areas of Glasgow.

I had no choice but to take it – and to be grateful for it too. I was paid less than I had been in my student job at the theatre.

As for the job itself: the scaffolders would call up and ask to be put through to the foreman, and I'd invariably cut them off. When they called back, I'd do it again.

Even a self-taught Commodore 64 user like me struggled to adjust to manning phone lines with quite such ease. People would get annoyed, and I'd spend most of my time apologising for having cut them off, muttering something about how the line had been on the blink all day.

The most difficult thing to handle though, was that I was recognised as "her off the telly" by the guys at the company, and by the stream of scaffolders who would come into reception.

I felt humiliated. There was no shame in doing the job itself, but the hard part was having to laugh off remarks about me being "old news". 'This is a bit of a fall from grace, isn't it love?'

This successful and fairly well-known TV presenter had become a washed-up has-been. A "one-minute wonder".

It's an all too familiar story to most people who have ever worked in the TV industry. The free-flowing offers of work that had come so readily had simply dried up. Once, I hadn't even had to try to get work, in fact, my schedule had been so crammed, I'd actually had to turn work down. But then, suddenly, I couldn't buy another TV job.

My agent and I had been used to speaking every day. But that stopped too. There was nothing to discuss. There were no contracts to be negotiated, no personal appearances to be confirmed, and no signs of anything changing.

My parents, my sisters ... they had been so proud of my achievements. But now? What now? What did they tell their friends when they asked why they didn't see me on the telly anymore?

What I couldn't see back then was that they were still proud of me. Their love was (and is) unconditional. It was never defined by the work that I did or didn't do.

So, all those years ago, my extraordinary family got together and decided I needed a holiday. A change of scene. They could see I was really struggling, and they must have been worried that I was heading for another breakdown.

My sister and her family were heading off to Spain for Easter and very kindly asked me to join them. Mum and Dad paid for my flights, the accommodation came courtesy of my sister, and even I managed to scrape together enough pesetas for some tapas.

You know the rest ...

A few days into the holiday I was standing thigh deep in the sea, clutching my bottle of Valium.

I had taken the pills to Spain quite innocently. The doctor had prescribed them to help with my anxiety. Almost as soon as we landed in Spain though, a plan began to form in my mind. I was in a deep depression which a few days in Spain was not going to lift.

I feel as if somebody, somewhere was watching over me when I made that last-minute decision to live. To turn around and step out of the sea. To resolve to take the next steps forward in my journey.

I had no idea where that journey was going to take me next. Could I ever find happiness or at least some stability in my life?

The answer? Not for a long time to come.

CHAPTER 11

A CURE?

On my return from Spain I was still gainfully unemployed, so I signed back up with the temping agency.

I still didn't get placed in my jet-set PA role, but the job that materialised was a marked improvement on the last. Once again, I was to be a receptionist, this time in a small, family-run printing company. I actually enjoyed it. But that's wholly down to the fact that I met Jacqu.

Jacqu and I hit it off immediately and, at the time of writing, we've been the closest of friends for 15 years. She worked in the sales team. In fact, she was the sales team. It was a one-woman department. Her office was immediately off my little reception area, which, as it turned out, was ideal for our incessant chatting. (Incessant from me anyway. In fairness to Jacqu, she knuckled down to her work, despite my best efforts to distract her.)

Even in my second receptionist job, I still had that knack of cutting the callers off. Somehow, I still hadn't grasped how to use a phone system. But at least that gave me plenty of time to chat with Jacqu. Happy days! Well, for a little while …

My job in the printing company was only ever temporary and came to an end after a few months. Once again, I was unemployed and up against it financially. And it didn't take long for me to sink into yet another deep depressive low. This one was bad.

For the first few days, I sat at home, incapable of doing anything. Even drink and drugs held no interest for me. I couldn't see any light at the end of the tunnel. I was just sick of being in the bloody tunnel! Even a reckless and frightening hypomanic episode would have been light relief from this blackness.

My anxiety levels were at an all-time high. I had plenty of real worries, like my lack of work and impending inability to pay my mortgage. Then there were all the unnecessary anxieties, like whether or not the clear shoe boxes I had bought were actually the best way to organise my shoes.

Should I take a polaroid picture of each shoe to stick on the end of the box, so that I could see immediately where to find each pair? Tricky one, that. In the end, it went onto the "too-difficult" pile, but it still caused me no end of stress.

I was overwhelmed by everything.

Even when I had to drag myself from my bed to the toilet, I felt like I was walking through tar, with the energy of a lazy orangutan. They're the animal equivalent of a human couch potato apparently. Who knew?

Getting up in the morning was almost impossible. It was like raising the Titanic. But why would I bother to get up anyway? What was the point? Nothing mattered any more.

Showering and washing my hair? Absolutely out of the question. Even dry shampoo was too much of an effort.

At the other end of the day, the routine of cleansing my face and brushing my teeth was so daunting that I put off going to bed for a couple of nights in favour of staying on the sofa.

I was lost, lonely, desperately sad, and utterly exhausted.

I was empty and weak. I cried so hard inside but was too numb to cry real tears.

I wished I was dead.

I didn't get to the stage of making a plan. Let's face it, I'd had the ideal opportunity in Spain, and hadn't gone through with it. Thoughts of how it would break my family were still at the forefront of my mind.

I was paralysed with frustration. I couldn't die, but I couldn't do anything else either. Why was I alive? What was my purpose? What did I add to anything or anyone on earth?

This was desperate. Given any longer on my own, the suicidal ideations were only going to gather momentum. I had to find something else. So, I called my GP.

Remarkably, I got an appointment. Not for three-months-and-a-day-come-Tuesday, but for 11.30am. 11.30am that very same day.

It was already 10.45am. I smelt. My hair was, frankly, disgusting. I was wearing the same pyjamas I'd worn for the last 72 hours. At least 72.

Hmm. I was depressed though. It would be okay, wouldn't it? Depressed people are all lazy, and mope around, while everyone else just gets on with it – that's what people say. But no. I may have been contemplating suicide, but I couldn't sit in the doctor's surgery smelling. And wearing my pyjamas.

I had the merest flirtation with the shower, but it was enough to freshen me up.

Leaving the flat was just plain weird. I had that all too familiar feeling of not actually being present in my own life. I put one foot in front of the other and got to the surgery, but the whole thing was like an out-of-body experience.

Ten minutes later, I was back out on the street and walking back to the flat. That ten minutes had included a seven-minute wait to be called in to see the doctor.

My three-minute consultation hadn't gone quite the way I had hoped it would.

I'd seen the doctor once before. Nothing to do with mental health on that occasion, but I had remembered thinking she had picked a surprising career given that she exuded all the warmth of a frozen chicken. On the evidence of our second meeting, that first experience hadn't been a one-off.

After establishing that I didn't actually think I'd kill myself that afternoon, she advised that she wouldn't be able to refer me for any specialist care. At least not on that day. She'd write to the mental health team who would add me to the waiting list and I'd be seen in due course. It could take months though. She said I shouldn't hold my breath.

I got back to the flat and the silent tears that had been rolling down my face on the walk home took on a life of their own. I cried inconsolably. This was one brick wall that not even my steel wrecking ball could break down.

Surely someone, somewhere, with all their medical expertise could magic me into a normal, balanced person? Or at least not a suicidal liability?

I sat slumped on the sofa for hours. Even the TV became bored of the less-than-jolly environment and went into automatic standby mode.

Then I did it. I called Mum.

I was still crying, and stopping even for a phone call was beyond me. Within the space of an hour I was sitting in Mum's car and on my way to a private mental hospital. She'd called the hospital, and they had advised her that I'd need a referral.

It was out of hours. That posed no problem for Mum, who, in full-on superhero mode, found an out of hours GP practice who immediately referred me to the hospital. Twenty minutes later, I was hanging onto Mum's arm as she led me from the car to the rather grand hospital entrance.

I was about to spend the next six weeks there, leaving only twice. Once to go for a job interview, and the other to sneak out to the pub!

CHAPTER 12

HOTEL WITH A DIFFERENCE

I was taken straight up to see the psychiatrist – she must have seen truck-loads of patients like me, desperately seeking direction towards a better life. A life worth living. She didn't sound jaded though, just warm.

She asked – well, I don't mean to sound rude, but she asked all the usual questions. The questions I had first been asked by my GP all those years ago. I think I managed to get across the salient points.

Yes, I often felt low like this.

Yes, I had thought about taking my own life in the past.

Yes, I had gone as far as to make a plan.

Yes, I had ideations of suicide at the moment, but rather than kill myself, I'd opted to come here instead. To hospital.

She listened, without that distracting thing of taking notes, although it worried me that she might not remember what I'd said. It had taken all my energy to get the words out once.

The upshot of our chat was that I was to stay there for at least the next few days, to rest and recuperate, and to undertake some therapy sessions.

I'd also be put on a different antidepressant: citalopram, 60mg.

At that time, back in 2004, 60mg was the maximum dose. Since then, that's been cut to 40mg over concerns that higher doses may cause increased risks to the heart. (Bit alarming since I was on 60mg for eight years! Keep everything crossed for me.)

Then they showed me to my bedroom. Little did I know that it would be my home for the next six weeks.

It was nothing like any hospital room I'd ever been in before. It was more like a hotel room. It was carpeted. And not just any old carpet, a good quality soft carpet. I promised myself that I'd inspect it once the coast was clear, just to see if it needed the nail brush treatment.

There was a big, plush, double bed with subtly patterned linen. (There's nothing worse than a busy bedspread.) There was a dressing table with a large mirror, and a rather fancy-looking, wall-mounted TV. And there was a lovely big armchair, that I would curl up on for many hours, and gaze peacefully, yes peacefully, out of the window, onto the beautiful mature gardens.

The en suite bathroom was a little more "hospitalesque". I'd cope though. It was clean. I'd hold off asking Mum to bring in the bathroom cleaner and a cloth.

The main difference between this room and a hotel room was that there was no lock. Presumably this was so that patients couldn't lock themselves in and potentially harm themselves.

To be fair, all they'd have had to do was call Dad, who was of course an expert in breaking down doors thanks to my previous antics.

Mum and I waited for the nurse to come up and talk with me. It must have been so hard for Mum to see her troubled daughter in such a state. I had put them through so much over the years, and now I was a patient in a mental hospital.

As always though, she was stoic and practical. At least, on the face of it. I've got no doubt that she let her emotions spill out when she got home to Dad that night.

Mum made a list. Always a good thing to do in times of woe. Mum was scribbling down all the things she'd collect from my flat. Under normal circumstances, I'd have been all over that list. I'd have been working down from my head to my toes, as I always do when I'm packing. Shampoo and hair straighteners first, then I'd finish up with shoes. Oh, and jewellery. Passports and so on were on a separate list. Not that I'd need any travel documents during this particular mini-break.

On that evening though, I sat motionless. I stared into space, leaving Mum to make the executive decisions. I would probably only need a couple of pairs of knickers and a toothbrush to get me through a couple of nights. And bathroom cleaner. Knickers, toothbrush and bathroom cleaner.

I couldn't help myself. My only contribution to what I'd need was bathroom cleaner. Oh, and a packet of cloths. Perhaps I was in the right place after all.

The nurse arrived and sat down next to Mum. I was hunched up on the bed with my knees pulled close to my chest. She was just as warm and lovely as the psychiatrist. She explained that there was a lounge (and a smoking lounge) downstairs, plus a little kitchen to make coffee and tea.

There was even a full team of chefs who prepared homemade meals. Patients were encouraged to go for meals and mix with fellow patients. I'd soon wheedle my way out of that.

She asked whether I'd like to choose something to eat that evening. The dining room was closed for the night, but she would ask the chef to prepare me something light for my room. I will remind you, this was a hospital. Not a luxury five-star hotel.

The answer to whether or not I wanted food was a resounding no, but having noticed the pleading look on Mum's face, I opted for a plain omelette.

The nurse suggested I try to get some rest. She said the psychiatrist and my key worker would come up to talk with me in the morning, and left me to wait for my omelette.

Mum clucked around for as long as she could, until she eventually ran out of things to cluck about. Then she gave me a huge hug and a kiss and told me she'd be back in the morning.

It's only now, as I look back on that night, that I can really appreciate how horribly upsetting it must have been for Mum to leave me there. I'm crying right now, just thinking about it. I may have been 29 years old, but I was still, as she always says, her little girl.

My poor, poor mum. Once again, I'd caused her to feel sad and helpless. And I had, I'm sure, caused her to cry.

I remained on the bed for some time after Mum left. A strange feeling of peace came over me. I felt like nothing could harm me. I felt safe. Relieved. And possibly even optimistic that my few days in hospital would provide me with the tools I needed to feel sane.

Fingers crossed.

CHAPTER 13

MINOR BREAKTHROUGH

What? Group therapy? Talking to complete strangers?

Absolutely not. That was not happening. Not ever. Not in this lifetime.

Day one had started badly.

Mum had been in to deliver the essentials before the Michelin-starred hospital chefs had even written up the specials board. She'd put in a few other things too, but crucially, the bathroom cleaner and cloths had now reached the building.

After thoroughly cleaning my already sparkling en suite, I'd very bravely shuffled my way down to the kitchen to make coffee. I'd shuffled along to the meds room to get my meds. All 60mg of them. I'd located the smoking lounge, and had, so far, managed to avoid eye contact with everyone.

The lady assigned to be my key worker spotted me through the thick blue haze in the smoking lounge, and sat down with me to tell me what I could expect ...

I was given a timetable. There was cognitive behavioural therapy (CBT), relaxation, assertiveness and even art therapy. Plus, there was one-to-one therapy ... Oh, and group therapy too.

I was horrified. One-to-one therapy was difficult enough. But group? She reassured me that group therapy had been found to be the most effective intervention.

I went to group. I hated it. I said nothing. I used up an entire box of the strategically placed boxes of tissues, then legged it back to my room.

This was not going to work. Shame. I'd had such high hopes.

I rebelled against going to the dining room for lunch too, but got caught. My key worker tracked me down and tried to talk me round. Apparently, everyone had misgivings about group at first, but almost without exception, once they'd tried it, they went on to reap the rewards.

As it turned out, I fell into that category too. And, as it turned out, I would be partaking in group therapy for far longer than just a few days.

For the next six weeks, I experienced every extreme of emotion. I talked openly about my lifestyle. The highs. The lows. The OCD tendencies. The relationship I had with my family. The inappropriate relationships I'd had with men. My unhealthy attitude towards food. My fears for the future. The loneliness. Uncontrollable anger. Desperate sorrow. And the hedonistic highs.

At the time, I was convinced my days of substance abuse were a thing of the past, (that was wishful thinking) so we didn't address them. But at least I got everything else out there as honestly as I could.

In return, I learnt coping mechanisms. I found out that keeping a mood diary would help me to identify any patterns as they emerged in my fluctuating moods.

When going out socially, I learned to plan out, in advance, when I would arrive, and when I would leave. This would help with the anxieties I had about meeting people. There would be an end point in place, at a time that suited me.

There were oodles of charts and graphs to help break down my patterns of behaviour, including one on "catastrophising". And I still find that one helpful now to bring my mind into check when it's about to go off on one. When it tries to convince me that the worst scenario is inevitable.

It isn't inevitable.

Mentally I began to feel stronger every day. I hadn't had any hypomanic episodes or devastating lows while I'd been in the hospital.

There had been plenty of tears though, much soul searching, and long periods of sadness, but there were some surprisingly amusing times too. I think it was humour that got me through those six weeks. Gallows humour.

Finding that humour in unlikely places never took away from the gravity of the situation. But somehow, sitting in the smoke-filled patients' lounge with some seriously ill souls, and having a competition to see how many songs we could think of that had the word "crazy" in the title seemed fun.

I got 'Still Crazy After All These Years' by Paul Simon. Pleased with that.

There were also the side effects of my new meds to contend with. I got headaches and felt more tired than I'd ever thought possible.

And then there was the shaking. I could barely lift a cup of coffee without spilling it, such were my shakes. My legs would shake of their own accord too.

I lost loads of weight. Citalopram can affect your appetite. I lost a stone and a half (nine and a half kilograms in new money) in six weeks. Bearing in mind I was a healthy weight when I arrived in hospital, that was quite a significant loss. One of the therapists joked that she'd be sending me up to the Eating Disorders Unit if I lost any more weight.

Not the most sensitive of jokes.

The days and weeks rolled by. Then, one day towards the end of my treatment, I happened to spot an advert in the newspaper. Two of the biggest football teams in Scotland were about to launch their own TV channels. And they were looking for an anchor presenter for each. (For those of you who don't know, football in Scotland is massive.)

Now bearing in mind my circumstances, this may sound weird, but what the hell – I decided I would apply anyway. Days later I received a call asking me in for an interview for lead presenter on this new channel for one of Glasgow's Old Firm football clubs.

Now, it's true that I was a very different person to the one who had practically crawled into the hospital all those weeks ago, but the prospect of going for an interview was still a tall order. And the afternoon before my interview I was nervous. Not just about the interview itself. I was also nervous about being out of the secure environment where I'd spent the past few weeks. I had become so used to being almost institutionalised, that the thought of stepping foot out of the lush, green hospital grounds was terrifying.

I missed dinner that night in favour of reading up on the latest goings-on in football, but was in such a tizzy that I didn't take anything in. So, I decided I needed a drink, but not one of the drinks on offer in the hospital kitchen ...

It was around 5.30pm and most people were still eating. I wasn't on any kind of lockdown in the hospital, so I signed myself out for a walk. What I omitted to say was that I'd be walking straight down the steep, tree-lined avenue to the local pub for a large vodka and tonic.

It was bliss. I sat in a quiet corner fiddling on my phone, pretending to look busy, and made short work of my drink. I hadn't had any alcohol for weeks, so it made me feel very relaxed, very quickly. My head was spinning, and I could so easily have had another. Thankfully, common sense prevailed (for once). I stopped at one and made my way back to the hospital.

When I got back to my room, I cleaned my teeth at least 25 times, in case any of the staff popped in for anything and smelt the alcohol on my breath.

They didn't. I got myself ready for bed, fully expecting a sleepless night given my nerves about the next day. But, probably due, in no small part, to my large vodka, I slept soundly that night and awoke feeling fresh for my interview.

The interview went well, and to my utter disbelief, I was offered the job.

I had managed to engage autopilot, and must have come across as a picture of health and wellbeing. Little did they know that I was on day release from a mental hospital, and would be heading straight back there afterwards.

The following week I was discharged from hospital. I was due to start my new job in just two weeks.

I was well, I thought. I was ready. And I was armed with my mental wellbeing toolbox, the instructions for which were in my lever arch files.

I had this nailed. Or so I thought.

But there was still a nagging doubt. I'd been waited on hand and foot for six weeks. I hadn't even had to think about the outside world. With hindsight, I think that was a bad thing.

But the bigger problem was that I had still only been treated for half the problem. Depression.

My gremlin was still alive and well. Undiagnosed and unchallenged.

As it turned out, my stay in hospital hadn't been the total cure I had hoped for. More of a minor breakthrough.

CHAPTER 14

CAREERING AHEAD

Over the following three years as I careered my way through my early thirties, work took flight once again.

Presenting the football channel was my regular weekday job. For five nights a week, I fronted the flagship show with one of the former high-profile players as my guest.

I had done good work on dealing with depression in hospital, but my mood swings were as extreme as they'd ever been. My emotions were always magnified in one direction or another. Both the highs and the lows were far more frequent and more intense than ever before.

There were days when I would get up at 5.30am to go for a run, come back, and spend half an hour doing an abdominal workout, then spend at least two hours showering and getting ready for work.

I would put a lot of thought into what I'd wear. It was a very precise science, and went right down to my belt, bag and purse, which had to match. It was a very meticulous process.

As for the lingerie, that was integral to the entire ensemble. It would need to be the same colour as whatever dress or top I was wearing, which meant that I had a pretty well-stocked lingerie drawer to cover all bases. Clearly, the knickers and bra were always a matching set.

On days like those, I would stride into work feeling on top of the world, and ready to embrace whatever the day had to throw at me. I felt in control. But the truth is, it was a false control. I was midway through a hypomanic episode, and with that came an insatiable need to talk to every single person in the building, from the work experience girl to the Head of Programmes.

I'd talk quickly, leaping from one line of conversation to another, all in the same breath. There were times when I was aware of my behaviour, but that only prompted me to talk more, in a vain effort to prove to myself and to others, that I was okay. I was in control.

That word again: control was a fundamental element of those hypomanic spells.

One day sticks out. I had tried on a couple of different outfits. One was a black dress, which, of course, called for black lingerie, and the other option was black leather trousers with a dark grey top. Cue the grey lingerie.

I'd spent so long faffing around that I lost track of time, and had to get a wiggle on if I was to get to work on time.

I settled on the black dress.

However, in my haste to get out the door, I had forgotten to change back into my black bra. It wasn't until I got to work that I realised I was wearing black knickers and a grey bra.

I froze. This was serious. My whole day was ruined. There was no way I could go live on air wearing mismatched lingerie.

I ploughed through the day, presented the show that evening, but felt agitated. I had tainted my need for order and perfection.

In the clear light of day, even although I do tend to wear matching lingerie, I fully accept that to mismatch for a day is really not a catastrophe. And yet, when I'm so far into the hypomanic typhoon, it's earth shattering.

Shopping was a feature of my hypomania too. Clothes and household items mainly. It wasn't so much that I quite fancied getting a new pair of hipster jeans, but that I needed them. And I needed them *immediately*. Then when faced with numerous options of which hipsters to go for, I'd invariably end up buying several pairs.

"Everything to excess." How right Dad had been when he'd said that all those years ago.

In complete contrast, there were other days when I would haul myself out of bed, pull on any old clothes, irrespective of whether they looked good or not, tie my hair up and mope into work. I would find it difficult to engage with people, and would dread doing the show, as it all seemed so overwhelming. Then, as soon as the director said that we were off air, I'd be out of the studio like a shot, so I could whizz back to the safety of my flat.

It was a tall order to succeed in the job with all that chaos going on, both professionally and personally. And, on the subject of men ...

I was a serial dater, and more often than not, chose to date the wrong kind of man. The sort of men who would never understand my mental health, but who were powerful in some way.

Deep down, I craved emotional and physical security, so was subconsciously drawn to men who I felt could look after me.

Emotional security because I was clearly incapable of securing my own emotions. Physical security because I had been in a physically abusive relationship. It had gone on for a year, but years afterwards, I still wasn't over it.

I'm well over it now, but after a year of being kicked, punched and thrown across the room, it took a while. The animal even had the foresight to keep the visible signs of his violence to below the neck. So, there were never any visible signs of abuse, unless I was naked. Which generally speaking, in public, I was not.

Only my mum ever saw the bruises, and that was on the day the relationship ended, when I had sold my flat and moved back home for a short time.

I had nightmares for years; I still do, sometimes. But it's okay. Many therapy sessions – and a lot of soul searching – helped. I had to find peace with myself as much as anything, because I felt a weird mix of guilt and anger. Guilt, because I had convinced myself I deserved to be abused. Anger (at myself), because I couldn't believe I'd been so weak to allow it to go on for so long.

Now, finally, I know it wasn't weakness that forced me to endure the trauma for so long. It was far more complex than that. And if you've ever been in a situation like it, you'll know, only too well, how complex the emotions and attachments are.

Complex or not though … Take a stand. Get out. Abuse of any kind is unacceptable.

The first step is to be honest with yourself and admit that you are in an abusive relationship. The next step, and the hard one, is to take action.

It's difficult. Really difficult. Frightening, in fact. But however hard it is to take that action, you must.

You CAN find your freedom again. And you deserve it. We all do.

So, with all of that going on, I did often wonder how on earth I made it all work. But I must have been doing something right … During my time presenting the football show, I was also invited to present my own property programme. This combination of jobs helped push me back in the public eye, and into the newspapers. Mainly for good reasons. Sometimes not.

There was one particularly uncomfortable story about my current boyfriend and I getting more than a little amorous on the balcony of my flat. Much of the story was a gross exaggeration of the truth, but to the everyday reader, I probably would have sounded like some kind of racy exhibitionist.

Most embarrassing.

The most frustrating thing was never getting to the root of where those stories came from. Just where was that paparazzi photographer hiding?! But while I may not have been the harlot

I was made out to be in that exposé, I could never profess to being saintly in other areas of my life.

Drink and drugs were back on the scene in a big way, albeit only ever after work hours.

I was always searching for the next high. Sometimes I found it in the misguided excitement of dating a wannabe gangster. Other times I found it through drinking to excess or taking cocaine.

Speaking of "searching", it reminds me of one particularly desperate night of multitasking in my flat. I was making a coffee on one side of the kitchen worktop and cutting a gram of cocaine on the other.

I used to cut the entire gram and decant it into a little pillbox, so that I didn't need to go through the whole pantomime of cutting every time I fancied a toot. I would just sniff it up through a short straw.

Calamity number one: I spilt the coffee granules on the floor. But instead of cleaning up the coffee straightaway, I went back to clearing up all the remaining cocaine powder from the worktop to get it safely into the pillbox.

Unfortunately, there was more clumsiness to come. Somehow or other, having just snapped the pillbox shut, I managed to drop it on the floor. Calamity number two.

It happened in slow motion. I think I hit the ground before the box did, to check that it was still intact.

It wasn't. The box had popped open, spilling all the cocaine onto the floor, in amongst the bloody coffee granules.

I wailed out loud! A whole gram!

The light in the kitchen wasn't great and it was beginning to get dark outside. Not to be thwarted, I thought quickly and got a torch so that I could see exactly where it was on the laminate floor.

Everywhere was the answer.

So, the floor was now sporting a brown and white speckled covering, and I was practically breathing into a paper bag panicking about how I could salvage the white stuff. I got two credit cards and scooped up as much of it as I could, but it was now mixed in with coffee granules. I spent the next half-hour painstakingly separating the two. I did not a bad job, but the cocaine was now pale brown in colour. And smelt of coffee.

There was still a fair bit of the drug in the laminate grooves. I couldn't bear to waste it by sweeping it up. So, I lay down on the floor on my tummy, shoved a straw up one nostril, and went about systematically sniffing it out of every groove.

Goodness knows what else I shoved up my nose from the floor that got walked on every day, but in my desperate state, it had to be done.

The remainder of the gram which I'd salvaged was just plain weird. It resembled a very dark shade of bronzing powder. I'm sure it gave me a better high than normal though, as I was getting a mix of cocaine and caffeine. As I always say, in every bad situation comes some good.

But seriously, not cool, and a sure-fire sign that I was far too fond of this drug.

Later, I found out that more than 50 per cent of people with bipolar have a history of substance abuse or dependency. It's often used as a means of trying to control the extreme symptoms, particularly before diagnosis, when you don't know how else to treat it.

Sometimes though, it's believed that drug use is specifically used to induce extreme states. That makes sense to me.

When in the midst of a deep depressive low, taking cocaine would feel a bit like a hypomanic state. For me, it was a temporary escape from the pain of depression; from the everyday torment of trying to live with, and conceal, a serious mental illness.

I just couldn't see it at the time, but all those things were taking me further and further away from finding a meaningful and happy life.

Living with the secret of my mental illness played havoc with work at times. The fear of opening up, just because of the stigma surrounding mental illness, only served to compound the symptoms.

If I'd had a migraine, I would have called the producer to let him know, and would no doubt have been wished a speedy recovery, and told to return to work when it cleared up. But in the throes of a severe depressive low, when I was unable to function, the lack of general understanding (or acceptance) of mental illness meant that I'd make up all sorts of excuses to prevent me from going to work ...

I cited more migraines than is humanly possible.

I solemnly announced that I had to go and visit family members who had become seriously ill. Given the varying severity of the "illnesses", the visits sometimes lasted for a few days.

On one occasion, I elaborately explained that my car had been vandalized. It hadn't. I explained how I had to stay at home until the windscreen repairman arrived to replace the smashed window. And then he ended up arriving at 4.00pm, so it wouldn't be worth my while coming into work for such a short time.

I even used the excuse of losing my voice. As luck would have it, I genuinely had lost my voice in the past, so it posed no problem to give my boss a rundown (by email, as I couldn't speak) on how I'd been struck down by this dreadful affliction.

Sadly though, in feeling the need to hide the real reason for not being able to go to work, it left me feeling even more alienated than I already was.

I used to feel like a complete and utter misfit. I felt battered, bruised, vulnerable and alone. And guilty. I hated the lying and the deception.

Something had to change. And if I couldn't change the way I was feeling, maybe I could change something else ...

After three and a half years of presenting the Old Firm football channel, I was invited down to London to present on a now defunct sports news channel. I still find it incredible that despite my monumental mood swings and erratic behaviour, I was being offered work. It was a rolling news channel, and I was to co-present the breakfast show.

This was huge. London! The streets were paved with gold down there, weren't they?

It was one thing to have built up a bit of a name for myself in Scotland, but to live and work in London was what I'd always dreamt of.

I jumped at the chance. And, as with everything in television, it happened very quickly. Two weeks after having been offered the job I had packed up my flat, stuck up a 'To Let' board, scooped up my two chihuahuas, and driven 400 miles to where my new life would begin.

This was it. This was my chance to start all over again. My chance to forge out a balanced and responsible life. Nobody would know about my previous ups and downs, and the new 'London me' would be the epitome of balance.

Everything in moderation.

Easy.

CHAPTER 15

UNACCOUNTABLE

I took to life in London well.

For the first few months, I was so busy settling into my new role as presenter of the breakfast show that I had little time for anything else. Little energy too, given that I had to get up at 4.00am, five days a week. I constantly felt as though I had jet lag.

It was a good time though. I loved the vibrancy of living in London, and there was a good bunch of people working on the channel.

My social life began to take off within the first few months. And it took off in style.

I began dating a guy who treated me like royalty. It wasn't a one-way thing though. I liked him. He had a good heart. He introduced me to all the best restaurants and clubs. There was VIP treatment everywhere we went. This guy was well connected and well respected. He had a ticket to anything and everything he wanted.

Including cocaine. There was a lot of it. And lots of cocaine meant lots of all-night benders.

On a couple of occasions, we went to a small private members' club and the manager would take us into his office for a sneaky line or two.

But, the best, or rather, the worst, was yet to come.

One night, when we got back to his very posh penthouse apartment, having been in the front row at a Chris Rock concert, the cocaine appeared, and quickly disappeared. All but a gram.

Eventually, I decided I had to sleep. I'd been partying constantly for days, and my body and mind were crying out for rest. We took a sleeping pill to try to counteract the amphetamine effect of the cocaine. Ten minutes later though, we decided to get back on it and polish off that final gram.

It was the biggest mistake we could have made.

The hallucinations were vivid ... I remember creeping around the apartment opening countless wardrobe doors, looking for people. I was convinced my friends were hiding out, ready to jump out with balloons and party poppers as a surprise for me.

At one point I asked my boyfriend whether the people in one of the wardrobes were his friends or mine. I couldn't make head nor tail of what was going on. I opened one door and closed it again, to seriously contemplate why that person should be wearing a cap indoors.

Taking recreational drugs on their own was one thing, but mixing them with other chemicals was just beyond stupid. Thankfully, we made it through to the morning and the effects of our cocktail of drugs wore off.

I reckon that was a close call to becoming really ill though. In an absurd kind of a way, I believe I was lucky that night. It wasn't the first time I had the sense that someone, somewhere was looking out for me.

Our relationship couldn't last.

Firstly, and most importantly, I began to doubt my feelings for him. But secondly, and quite surprisingly given my need for a high, I wanted to try to rein in the unsustainable social life that went with it. Moderation, remember? That was the new me.

Relationship number one was done and dusted. Next!

An all-too-familiar pattern emerged. Just like my Glasgow days, I'd fall madly in love almost instantly, then fall out of love just as quickly.

I worked my way through countless men. Some were eligible, some didn't have a penny to their names, and some were very high profile, mainly in the world of football.

None of that mattered a jot though. It really didn't. I've always gone with my heart. And despite having had a flighty disposition, I was always true to myself, and never stayed with someone for the wrong reasons.

Yet for all my good intentions of wanting to curb my chaotic and at times drug-fuelled social life, every man I met seemed to like a taste of the high life. And with that, came champagne and cocaine.

To this day, I can't work out how I always ended up with the same type of man. I was like a beacon attracting men with "danger" tattooed on their forehead.

Like attracts like, perhaps?

My gremlin had come all the way to London with me, and was working full tilt to destabilise me. The highs of those back-to-back hedonistic nights were always followed by an almighty crash back into that dark pit of despair.

I knew why it kept on happening. I was earning well, and due to my unusual working hours, had loads of free time. Everything I wanted was easily within reach, just waiting for me to grab it.

At the heart of it though, was the fact that I was completely unaccountable to anyone. Least of all to myself.

CHAPTER 16

HOUSE PROUD

I often used to wonder: was my extreme behaviour a result of my poor mental health, or was it just a part of my personality?

When I was really happy, was that because I had a joyful disposition? When I was sad, was that because things really did suck? Or was it that I lived with a mental illness?

Over the years, I've come to the conclusion that there is a spectrum. A mood spectrum. It's a pretty simple concept. At one end of my spectrum it says, "very happy" and at the other end it says, "very sad". In between those extremes, you can fill it in with mood levels of your choice.

For example:

'A bit pants, but at least it's nearly the weekend.'

'Happy-ish, but I've still got a pile of ironing to do tonight which is pretty pants.'

'Pants' is the adjective of choice for me when it comes to mood. For me, it just says it all. You can use your own word. The mood spectrum will still work, I promise.

Every single person in the world is on my spectrum, and every single person in the world experiences high and low moods. We all feel ups and downs. The highs can feel absolutely brilliant!

For example, you wake up one Saturday morning and the sun is shining. You get dressed and discover you can fit into your skinny jeans again. Whoop, whoop! You celebrate by meeting a friend for a skinny latté. No hint of a double chocolate muffin on the side though, obvs, because you're a sizzling little hottie in those jeans and you've got a sexy little swagger going on.

Then, you go home and chill out in front of a good movie, put on a face mask, lay out your carefully co-ordinated clothes for tomorrow, and tuck yourself up in bed ready for another great day ahead.

That's lovely isn't it? You're happy for goodness sake! And that happiness can come from the simplest of things. If you know how to make the most of those everyday opportunities ...

I was 34 years old and living in a cute little Victorian terrace in Battersea. The sun was shining after a really dull and grey few weeks.

It was Saturday, and I wasn't working. (I don't work in the traditional sense any more, but, I still love Saturdays – they feel different, don't you think?)

I discovered I could fit into my cute little skinny jeans for the first time in ages. Today was a good day! I wanted to celebrate. So, what to do?

At first, I thought about meeting my friend for coffee and a catch- up. I hadn't seen her for a while. I'd been feeling pretty low and had been avoiding people.

Yes. Coffee.

But then I just happened to look out of my window into the teeny but very sweet little garden at the rear of my rented house. At first glance, it looked pretty good. I'd been looking after it in a kind of "I'm not a gardener but can randomly prune a poor unsuspecting rose bush" kind of a way.

But, oh my days! Before I knew it, I was out in the garden with my notepad and pen, making a list of exactly what I needed to wipe the floor in the 'Best Small Garden' category at Chelsea Flower Show.

Thoughts of friend and coffee abandoned, I saw that the trellis needed a few little repairs. Small nails and hammer on the "to buy" list. The roses looked okay, but was that a greenfly? Maybe not, but better safe than sorry. Greenfly spray on the "to buy" list.

The little bushes in the flowerbeds were all well and good, but surely I needed a bit more variety? A mixture of grasses, flowering shrubs, crocuses, tulips or pansies (whatever the heck was in season) and a couple of uplighters all went on the "to buy" list.

I could go on, and suffice to say, my "to buy" list went on to include the likes of garden tools, flower tubs, a barbecue, and new garden cushions.

(To put this into perspective, the garden measured around 4m by 4m, was entirely paved, and had raised brick borders on three sides. Oh, and crucially, it looked perfectly lovely as it was.)

Good. So that list looked pretty comprehensive. Pleased with that.

But … if the garden was going to look so very fabulous, then I would need to bring the house up to an equal standard.

(Let's just remind ourselves at this point that this was a rented house. Improving the value of my home was entirely irrelevant, given that I'd be handing it back to the jolly grateful owner at some point.)

I'm now on page three of my "to buy" list, and have added the likes of two cafetières (one small, one large), a set of pots and pans (mine didn't match the rest of the kitchen), an entire set of white towels (my oatmeal ones didn't match the bathroom), and a couple of faux fur throws.

Mother of Pearl! Why hadn't I done this before? What must people have thought when they'd been to the house? #Mortified!

There definitely wasn't going to be time for coffee with my friend. This stuff needed to be done and now. Off I went in my little black BMW Z3. The roof was down, and my freshly washed hair was blowing in my face. (Actually, it was mainly sticking to my lip gloss. Hate that.)

Garden centre shopping? Check.

Department store shopping? Check.

A couple of new sets of lingerie and a new pair of skinny jeans? Check.

Back into the little Z3, lip gloss now wiped off, and home to empty the completely overloaded car of my beautiful new things. Then, I set about transforming the house and garden.

(In case you're wondering, none of this frantic activity was fuelled by cocaine, but the high it induced was not dissimilar.)

By around 8.30pm everything was looking pretty darn good. I sat in the garden for at least one and a half minutes to savour its splendour.

I then took myself back into the house to relax on the sofa, with the new faux fur throw casually draped over the arm, to watch a chick flick.

Around 30 seconds later, I popped back out into the garden. Then back into the house to check that the new pots and pans were still sitting perfectly straight on their stand. I re-folded one of the fluffy white towels in the bathroom that was not quite square, then took myself back to the sofa.

My new lingerie! Best try that on. And best try on my entire wardrobe and do a good old clear-out while I'm at it.

Back to the sofa.

But what about the money I'd spent today? I hadn't worked that into my accounts. Was there going to be enough money on pay day to clear the card that had taken such a battering?

Money used to always be a source of enormous anxiety for me. As I knew only too well, working in TV was notoriously insecure at the best of times and although I'd generally been lucky, I could never be certain when the next job was going to present itself.

Even when I was earning well, the level-headed me was very good at living within my means to save money for any lean times. You'll notice I said the "level-headed" me. What I mean by that is, the me when I am well. Me in a hypomanic episode is a completely different thing. As you now know.

The truth is I had not been in a position to go on such a mammoth spending spree. I didn't have the money in the bank to pay off the credit card, and come pay day, there still wouldn't be enough, not after paying my extortionate London rent.

The thing is, hypomanic or depressive episodes manifest in different ways for everyone. My OCD tendencies had manifested through the endless lists and the need to strive for the absolute best. For perfection – a perfection that I would never find.

And what about spending money that I didn't have? It was as if I was living someone else's life. I knew I couldn't afford to buy those things, but I was on such a high that I thought, *what the heck* … On some level, I just thought I could deal with it. I could deal with anything!

The agitation and anxiety were exhausting. Even when my body and mind were crying out for rest, I simply couldn't settle. I would race from room to room with absolutely no purpose at all. Being still was not on the agenda.

Oh, and I never did see my friend, did I?

Instead, I spent the entire day alone, albeit talking at great length to every single person I came across. Shop assistants, people in the queue, people perusing the same area of the shop as me, and anyone else who would listen. Or not listen. They all got talked at.

We are all basically feeling our way through life, making the most of the joys, and coping with the challenges. I'm no different in that respect. The difference is that for me, the joys can sometimes become such extreme highs, that I spiral out of control, unable to find the pause button. I am unaware of reality.

I will focus on just one thing – like an African lion about to pounce on a zebra.

Or I will forget to eat. Or I will red-button anyone who calls, because if I don't get through my list, the world may just end.

Or I will call every single person I can think of and talk at them at a hundred miles per hour, for hours on end.

Or, and I'm so ashamed to admit to this, I will disregard the needs and feelings of my nearest and dearest if there's even the teeniest chance that they'll interrupt my hypomanic state.

For me though, the saddest and most tragic thing about that morning is that, having woken up with so much to be thankful for, my hypomanic state stole all the joy and happiness away.

The happiness I thought I felt was all fake. It had no substance. The day after that particular episode, I slumped into a devastating low which lasted for a couple of weeks.

I had debt to worry about.

I was even more isolated from friends and family than before.

I got absolutely no joy in wearing my wildly expensive new lingerie.

I didn't give a fig about the stupid cafetières.

I was more than sad. My body was filled with a heavy blackness that seemed to treble my body weight. Just walking from the bedroom to the bathroom was absurdly hard.

The loneliness was horrible. I wanted company, I craved it, but I couldn't call or speak to anyone.

I had to hide away from the world in which everyone else was living, laughing, crying, learning, growing and experiencing. That world of human experience felt like a remote, alien place, a million miles away from my existence.

In the space of a day, I had flown so far off my mood spectrum that I didn't even get a chance to experience the very happy end of the scale. By the next day, I was already on my way past "very sad" and I didn't stop until I was crawling into the abyss beyond.

Beyond was not okay.

I had reached that place where I had no reason left to live.

CHAPTER 17

A SPORTING MOVE

Eighteen months after moving to London, I was made redundant. We were all made redundant. The sports news channel had collapsed.

For someone who doesn't enjoy great stability at the best of times, that should have rocked me to the core.

In fact, it didn't.

Incredibly, the bosses at another major sports broadcaster had apparently been watching the news show I had been presenting. Everyone in the industry knew the channel was going to go under any day. One of the big bosses at this other channel had, for some reason, picked me out as a presenter he wanted to take on when the inevitable happened.

So, the day after being made redundant, I was walking across Wimbledon Common on my way to watch the tennis, with my then boyfriend. My phone rang.

I was hideously hungover after the commiseration drinks with my work colleagues the night before. The voice on the other end of the phone introduced himself. I knew his name very well.

Now, rather than taking a deep breath and preparing myself for whatever was going to come next, I replied with, 'Yeah, very funny. Who is this really?'

Everyone in the business knew this man, so to think that he'd be calling me was ridiculous. But he assured me he was who he'd said he was, then went on to invite me in for a chat.

Needless to say, I accepted his kind offer, and a few days later had landed myself one of the most prestigious jobs in football. I was to be the anchor presenter for football's Scottish Premier League.

I would be the first woman in history to have taken on this role. I would also do a bit of presenting on the company's news channel.

The whole thing was a bit surreal. Plenty of producers had demonstrated their faith in me in the past by allowing me to present their shows, but this? This was huge!

One of the most well-known and respected sports broadcasters had picked me – yes, me – to front one of the most well-known football leagues in the world. Audience figures would far exceed any of my previous shows. Scottish football has a cult following.

In theory, it should have been great ... but it didn't go well. In fact, it went heinously wrong.

The best way I can put it is to say that I didn't fit in. Through a sequence of events, I visibly crumbled as a presenter during my time there.

The frustration was that nobody watching at home could have known what I was up against. All they could see was a rather uncomfortable looking woman, like a rabbit in the headlights, as she clumsily discussed the teams that are so passionately followed by their loyal fans.

I turned into a nervous wreck on screen, which led to me getting some bad press for the first time ever. The balcony story was nothing compared to what was to come.

My ability as a presenter was called into question. The articles were vicious and personal. On one occasion, my dress was even ridiculed. A very expensive, red fitted dress which had been bought for me by the TV stylist.

It was painful. And I was mortified.

There was, however, one story that I have to take responsibility for. Given the fact that I had no confidence in the way I looked, I decided to get lip fillers. It was another means of getting a high. Such was my excitement though, that when the doctor had injected the fillers, I had a look, and asked for a little more. I wanted those babies to pout. And then, when she'd finished injecting, I asked her to fill up her syringe again and put even more in.

By the third time, she flatly refused to do it.

I presented the football as normal that weekend. The poor make-up artist must have had to restock on lip gloss after she'd made me up. She went through almost an entire tube to make any impact on my dramatically plumped-up lips.

The following day, I got a phone call from a friend, telling me that there was a story about me in one of the newspapers. Hopefully it would be something nice. Perhaps even a piece on how well I'd been looking on air. People would have known something was different, but wouldn't have been able to pin down exactly what had changed.

Oh, my days. Oh, my blooming days.

Ali looks a bit POUT of the ordinary.

Next to the headline was a close-up picture of my face. My lips were the star attraction. It was only then that I realised how ridiculously big they were. They were comedy!

I was badly in need of a confidence boost, but was just dealt another kick in the stomach. And it was of my own doing.

It was a horribly tough time for me. Work was miserable. Every weekend when I came off air, it would take the next two-to-three days to recover from the ordeal. As someone who had more live TV hours under her belt than most, this was absolutely unheard of.

I would cry. I would hide out in my little house in Battersea, and spend the next couple of evenings (or days, which ran into evenings), drinking, until the memory of the latest show became blurred.

I would be full of self-loathing. I would feel humiliated at having had to put myself up on the parapet once again, only to be knocked down.

At the end of the football season in May, my contract, not surprisingly, was not renewed.

There was absolutely no way on earth I would have accepted a new contract anyway. Even if it had been presented to me on a silver platter.

Once again, I was unemployed.

Unemployed with a huge monthly London rent to pay, and with no prospect of any work on the horizon. It will come as no surprise that I fell into a devastating depression.

I was so unable to function that I couldn't even begin my search for work. And all I could think of was, *here we go again* ...

PART II

2009

THE DIAGNOSIS

CHAPTER 18

HOPE SPRINGS ETERNAL

It's a day I will never forget. A day that changed my life beyond recognition. A beautifully sunny day, as it happens, but my soul was writhing in agony, back in the black hole where the sun never dared to shine.

I was 35 years old.

I was still living in London, and I was still out of work, living on the ever-depleting savings from the good times.

I had been in a deep depression for months and had just about reached the stage where I couldn't fight any more. Not surprisingly, I was beginning to discover that no amount of alcohol would piece me back together again. I was utterly done in.

Despite the best endeavours of the psychiatrists I had seen over the years, no one had managed to cure either my aching soul or my chaotic mind. To be fair, it would have taken a brave person to explore inside my head. It was absolute carnage in there. It should have come with a public health warning.

I was still taking antidepressants, and had of course had several bouts of intensive therapy, including my stay in the mental hospital in Glasgow, but nothing had had any lasting, positive impact on my mental wellbeing.

The main impact they'd had was to drain my poor parents of all their savings. The hospital fees had been extortionate, but Mum and Dad had wanted to do everything in their power to try to rescue their little girl. The little girl who had become an utterly miserable, pained young woman.

During that time when I was out of work, I was just existing, not living. I lurched from day to day, overwhelmed by anything and everything, and was incapable of functioning.

How heart-breaking it must have been for my parents to have to watch their daughter in this broken and hopeless state yet again.

Although I lived 400 miles away from them, they knew exactly what was going on. Mum always says she gets the "vibes". And she does! With alarming accuracy! However much I tried to feign balance and positivity, Mum always saw right through it.

Given that none of the medical support I'd had was working, I reached the conclusion that I was not ill. How could I be? If I was genuinely suffering from an actual medical condition, then pills and therapy would have helped. Wouldn't they?

The antidepressants did numb the pain a little, but they did nothing for the mayhem that was my mind. That bad boy was still dancing its merry jig, like fleet-footed Irish dancer, Michael Flatley, on acid.

Reluctantly, I had begun to accept that this was all "just me". I was absolutely all over the place, never knowing what mood would show up from one minute to the next. But I carried on telling myself, that was just my character. It was my personality. I was officially highly strung. Higher than Dubai's Burj Khalifa at times.

And if I wasn't ill, how could a doctor make me better? There was nothing to fix. This was it. Life according to Ali. Brilliant.

So, when that latest episode came on, I just wanted to give in to it. But somehow, I decided to give it one last throw of the dice. I made an appointment to go and see another psychiatrist in London.

I knew nothing about this lady, except that she consulted from the same group of private mental health hospitals in which I had been an inpatient. It was worth a shot, wasn't it?

Oh, my goodness! She was lovely! And so perceptive. Somehow, she knew just what questions to ask me in order to draw out the information I'd never been able to express before.

She asked about my low moods, but was also interested in the way I felt and behaved around my depressive spells. It was the first time I'd ever been asked about that.

At first, I wasn't sure how to describe the highs. Given that I'd never fully recognised them as being anything other than my excitable nature before, I had to think really hard to pinpoint them.

She slowly teased the information she needed out of me, without ever putting words into my mouth or making suggestions. She simply asked the right questions.

She spoke to me quietly for what seemed like hours, but I felt so safe and protected from the outside world that I didn't want to move.

I knew there was a bombshell coming when she gently moved to the edge of her chair to talk more intimately with me. Her voice stayed calm. She exuded a beautiful warmth and empathy.

As I looked at her, I felt such enormous admiration. She was dinky in stature. Very attractive, and immaculately turned out, with her own individual sense of style. Her skin was tanned, with a naturally olive complexion. She had shoulder length, wavy hair, and wore no make-up or nail varnish.

I took it all in, and decided I wanted to be her. This kind, compassionate woman was the person I wished I could be.

Of course, I knew I couldn't make any assumptions. I couldn't possibly know whether she was truly happy in life. Or whether she just cared so deeply about her patients that she could put her troubles to one side, while she focused on helping people in her consulting room.

I found myself hoping she was truly happy. That her life was all that she desired. She was deserving of that. What a beautiful spirit.

And then it came.

'Ali, you are suffering with a mental illness called Bipolar II.'

Boom! There it was.

I remember having what felt like an out-of-body experience. As I looked down, I could see the doctor talking to a sad and frightened young woman, who was listening to her every word, with tears rolling down her face. She looked like a small child rather than a 35-year-old woman.

There was something else though.

This sad figure's face had softened since she had first walked into the consulting room. There was a change, but what was it?

Relief. It was relief.

An overwhelming feeling of joyous relief that this long and complicated mystery may eventually have been solved.

As a teenager, I had read Vivien Leigh's biography. She was my idol. *Gone with the Wind* – a classic. My VHS video recorder used to stick because I'd watched it so many times. (I must watch it again actually. Give it a go if you haven't ever seen it.)

Vivien suffered from manic depression, which is now known as bipolar. That all popped into my head while I was sitting in the consulting room. I'd read so much about the actress's life, and how friends had described that she would appear absolutely normal, sometimes for weeks on end, but would then become a completely different person. Then, she would fly into a rage and be rude and hysterical, or manic and excitable, and wildly out of control.

Reportedly, the first sign that all was not well for Vivien was that she would unconsciously and systematically take off all her jewellery, and start compulsively cleaning. It all made sense. Why hadn't I seen it before?

I'd toyed with the notion that I might have been on the bipolar spectrum, but had always assumed it would have been picked up by one of the many medical professionals I'd seen.

I was young when I read Vivien's book, but the symptoms for me were still very much alive even back then. I reflected on my own experience: I was essentially a kind and thoughtful person, but then, in the blink of an eye, that bubble would burst. Loudly.

I would be desperately sad and tearful, thinking of nothing but my own pit of despair. I'd be frightened and overwhelmed. Angry. Exhausted and withdrawn. Unable to function in any way whatsoever.

At its worst, I'd have ideations of suicide.

But then, that black pit could suddenly be filled with a beautiful white light, and I'd become strong and utterly invincible. The same me, who couldn't even bring herself to shower one minute, was running full pelt down a steep hill, unable to control her pace, the next ... talking at a hundred miles an hour. Making endless lists. Not sleeping. Focusing with microscopic precision on one task.

Sitting there in the psychiatrist's consulting room, it sort of made sense that I had bipolar.

She went on to explain our proposed plan of action so that we could work at bringing my newly identified illness under control. It would be trial and error until we found the right balance of drugs. And there would be intensive therapy.

In a way, I wish I could turn the clock back to that snapshot in time in the consulting room, as I took in a lot less of what she said after the diagnosis.

I do remember the crying though. I was crying uncontrollably.

Had this woman with the beautiful spirit and energy found a cure to my excruciating pain?

The answer is that there is no cure for bipolar, but, with the right treatment, it can be managed.

On that day, on that sunny afternoon in London, my life changed. It quickly became unrecognisable from the life I had been living for 35 years.

Thank you, doctor. Thank you. You gave me a life.

Bipolar had tried, and still tries, to break me; to overpower me. It had tried to cut me off from the real world, leaving me to battle it out for yet another day. It had created the most lonely and isolating existence imaginable.

Nobody should feel that alone.

There would, I learnt, always be some seriously tough times to contend with along the way. But from that day on, I sensed that there was more to life than existing. I had a lot of living to do …

PART III

2009 – 2018

POST DIAGNOSIS

CHAPTER 19

ACTION PLAN

Just because I'd been given a name for my illness, I still felt sceptical about whether I would actually feel any better. But, in the days and weeks that followed my diagnosis, the depression lifted, and I felt a renewed sense of purpose.

For as long as I could remember I had been suffering with these extreme mood swings. It was all I had known. So, could my quality of life really improve with a few pills and yet more therapy?

I figured I may as well give it a bash. Nothing ventured nothing gained. Plus, I didn't want to upset my lovely psychiatrist by shunning her help.

But if I were to believe in this diagnosis, I still felt like I needed to know why it had gone unchecked for so long. How come, having been under the care of so many professionals, nobody had managed to identify what was actually going on with me?

I've felt angry about that, many times. I've thought about how different life would have been if I had been treated appropriately, much sooner. All the pain and the suffering that this devastating illness had inflicted over the years could have been massively reduced.

That's not a particularly helpful exercise though, is it? So, I try not to dwell on it.

What I find incredible though, is that it takes an average of ten and a half years to receive a correct diagnosis of bipolar in the UK. Ten and a half years! Staggering.

Not only that, but before it's diagnosed you're likely to receive an average of three and a half misdiagnoses. Those statistics were reflective of my story, only it took far longer than ten years before I got my correct diagnosis.

But at least I got there in the end. And, I was ready to embrace the action plan as set out by my intuitive psychiatrist. The first step was to identify which drugs would (hopefully) work for me.

I was still on the highest dose of the antidepressant, citalopram. This, remember, was still some years before the UK drug regulator lowered the maximum dose to 40mg.

I was also prescribed a mood stabiliser called lithium. Bleurgh! I didn't like it one little bit.

While we were adjusting the dose to try to find the right amount for me, I needed to have blood tests every two months to check the lithium levels, and to check my kidney and thyroid function. That was a pain, and I certainly didn't enjoy giving blood, but the real reason the doctor took me off lithium was that the side effects became too much.

I was ridiculously tired all the time, my mouth was drier than the desert, no matter how much water I'd drunk, and my legs became stiff and achy. I felt light-headed, and with all the water I'd been drinking, I needed to pee all the time. Worse than that though, I began to lose control of my bladder!

That was not a good situation. Not a good situation at all. I really wasn't ready to embrace a life with incontinence pants just yet!

With bipolar meds though, it's very much a case of tailoring the combination of drugs to suit each individual. We're all made up differently, so while lithium works brilliantly for some people, it just wasn't right for me. So, we tried a 250mg dose of a mood stabiliser called lamotrigine.

It was another life changer, and I don't say that lightly. It worked brilliantly for me. It still does

To complete the cocktail of drugs, we tried me on an antipsychotic called aripiprazole. I started on a very low dose of 5mg, but in conjunction with the other two, it seemed to work well.

I'm still on this drug combination today, and I always will be.

My initial scepticism over whether my mood swings could ever be brought under control, or at least reduced, was slowly beginning to fade.

For some people, the very act of taking all these drugs is a bit scary. And, as we've learnt from the change in regulations for citalopram, and as with most drugs, they are not without their risks. I get that.

Plus, in taking these meds, it forces us to accept that we are mentally ill. That's a huge hurdle for many of us to overcome.

And there is still a real stigma attached to taking drugs for a mental illness. I get that too.

For me though, I practically grab my bag of goodies from the pharmacist's hands when I go to collect my repeat prescription. They're my lifeline.

It wasn't always like that though. Way back in the early days when I had to go to the pharmacy for my repeat prescription of Prozac, I was embarrassed by it. I accepted my prescription sheepishly and felt sure the girls in the chemist would all talk about me being a "mental head" as I sprinted out of the shop wearing my wig and dark glasses for disguise.

Well, not really, but only because I didn't actually own a wig.

Oh, and I'm sure the girls did no such thing. Sorry girls, I should have thought more of you.

The way I see it, people living with diabetes need insulin to give them what their body doesn't produce. I need my meds to give me the chemicals that my brain doesn't produce.

It would take several years before I reached the stage of having no qualms at all about taking my meds. But I knew that my whole outlook towards mental illness had to change. Whereas once it was my biggest secret, I was ready to stand tall and emerge from my bipolar closet.

I would never go out of my way to crowbar it into every conversation. That would just be weird. Nor would I shy away from mentioning it, any time it felt appropriate.

The meds were just one side of the story. I had counselling too – and for the first time ever, it really helped. We covered loads of subjects, some directly and others indirectly linked to bipolar.

We identified how I would recognise the early warning signs of a depressive or hypomanic episode. We dealt with the enormous sense of guilt I carried surrounding the hell I'd put my parents through over the years.

We also dealt with my alcohol intake. When the therapist asked me how much I was drinking, I was honest. I told him that I was drinking more than a bottle of wine a night, sometimes far more, and that yes, it affected me during the day. I told him that, in fact, it wasn't unusual for me to start drinking in the afternoon.

Our conversation didn't need to go very far before he suggested that perhaps I might just want to consider going to an Alcoholics Anonymous meeting. Actually, I think he'd have marched me there right there and then if he could have. He was fairly insistent that I ought to go.

I was gobsmacked.

Alcoholics wake up in the morning and reach for a bottle of vodka. They smell of alcohol and steal in order to fund their habit. Right?

In for a penny, in for a pound ... So, along with my new meds and counselling, I took myself off to AA.

I cried through the whole of that first meeting. I couldn't believe I had allowed my drinking to get so out of control, and what's more, I hadn't even been able to see it happening.

Everyone I met at AA was so friendly, and there was a beautiful feeling of peace and serenity in the room. So much for the vodka-addled kleptomaniacs I'd been expecting,

Everything that goes on in an AA meeting is confidential, so I'll not go into it in any more detail here. But I can say that I went to a few meetings, and then decided to try to bring things under control on my own.

It's not that I was in denial. I knew, and had accepted that I had a problem, and that I had all the credentials to go to the meetings, but I wanted to try facing this demon myself.

With hard work, I managed to do just that. My treatment for both alcohol and drugs came from within. That doesn't make me any kind of a hero, but put simply, I got tired of it all.

I got tired of feeling physically unwell every day due to my excesses. I got tired of chasing happiness, when quite clearly, I was like a thoroughbred galloping full pelt down the wrong racetrack.

I just got tired.

There was still the physical craving for drink and that was hard to overcome. Really hard. And I'm pretty certain I kept elderflower cordial manufacturers in business for a while. I missed the euphoria of taking drugs too, but I got through it.

I guess everyone who has abused drink or drugs has a different story to tell. Everyone's perception of what constitutes addiction is different. But a bit further down the line, after a long period of abstinence from drink, I found that I could have the odd drink without falling back into the cycle of binge drinking. I really don't tend to enjoy drinking any more, but it's good to know that if I do ever fancy one, I can do it without fear of it getting out of hand.

I'm generally the dedicated driver on a night out – just like I used to be. And I enjoy it.

I do confess to drinking at least one 1.75 litre bottle of Coke Zero every day, but although that's clearly a different kind of unhealthy addiction, I'll allow myself that vice. For now.

So, I was in therapy, and this time, the therapy was dealing with the right illness. That was a very good start. I was on the right meds too, and that meant I was in a better frame of mind to listen, and to understand. I had a sense of calm, and perhaps most significantly, was desperate to learn.

I soaked up every single minute of our hour-long conversations. Now that I was on my new-found path towards a better life, I wanted to know every little detail that might help me along the way. It was early days in my journey, but with the promise of something resembling normality at the end of the path, I was determined to be the standout scholar.

My mindset had changed so much. I started to see myself as one of the lucky ones. I had found a combination of drugs that suited me. Sometimes the side effects are miserable, but they are manageable.

I learned to accept that I would be on a hefty dose of medication every day for the rest of my life, but I was grateful for it. The drugs did work – but they still weren't a cure.

I learnt that I would still dip my toe in the water of hypomania and depressive lows from time to time. And I was okay with that. The wild mood swings would be on a far milder scale than they had been before.

Once, I would have fully immersed myself in that pool of water, and struggled to stay afloat for days on end. But for the new me, it felt like more of a paddle. I would barely need to dry my feet afterwards.

Every cloud ...

CHAPTER 20

INTERNET DATING

I was 36 years old – a year into my shiny new life, post diagnosis. It used to be that I'd wake up every day with a sense of dread, never knowing what the gremlin had in store for me. But after the diagnosis, that fear dissipated. I was gradually gathering belief that the extreme mood swings, which I'd experienced for as long as I could remember, would be manageable.

Work had picked up again too.

I'd got a job presenting the weekly flagship show on one of the most successful football clubs in the Premier League, so travelled up from London to Manchester every Friday.

I had also started to present the early morning national news. This wasn't sports-related, it was general news.

As far as the football job was concerned, they had called my agent specifically to ask me to present the show, which gave me a much-needed confidence boost after my previous job.

As for the national news, I had approached them, and was delighted when they offered me some shifts on a freelance basis.

I thoroughly enjoyed both jobs, and was once again back to my old self on TV. I felt capable and composed.

I'd start as soon as the 10.00pm news programme came off air, so would arrive at the studio at 10.30pm, and finish around 10.00am the following day. It was quite a shift.

It's often assumed that newsreaders simply arrive at the studio to read the news and then go home again, but in fact the job is far more involved than that.

You need to keep across all the big news stories as they are unfolding, and work closely with the producer to make sure the script works both for you and editorially. Plus, it's important that there's always a newsreader in the building to cover any breaking news.

I would often present the news on a Friday morning, so I'd get into London at 10.30pm on the Thursday, work through the night, present the early morning news, and then head off to the station to catch a train to Manchester for my other TV job. And then home to bed? Not always. It wasn't at all unusual for me to come off air in Manchester, jump back on a train, and head straight back to the London studio for another night shift.

It was a crazy schedule, but I always leapt at the chance of work when it came up.

In fact, I enjoyed it. Too much time on my own had never been a good thing. That is when the anxiety takes over, sadness creeps in, and before I know it, I'm on the downward spiral towards darkness. Either that or I have an explosion of energy which can lead to a frantic hypomanic episode. Neither is great, and both leave me feeling quite befuddled.

I'd sleep for two hours on the train, to and from Manchester, setting my phone alarm to make sure I didn't stay sleeping while the train turned around to go back in the opposite direction ... Except for maybe that one time! (Just the once in a period of several years though.) And bearing in mind just how little sleep I was getting, I don't think that's bad going.

In my previous life, that sort of schedule would have floored me. I may have turned to cocaine to keep me going, and would have expected to have had several bouts of depression. But having reached the stage where I wanted neither cocaine nor alcohol to govern my life, they didn't. And my meds worked wonders at helping me to cope with the testing work schedule.

My feelings of depression never reached a stage where I wanted to make a swift exit from the world, but there were still dark times, and I remember one night in particular: I was making my way into the news studio on a dark and miserable night. The rain was bouncing off the pavements, and I couldn't stop crying.

I wanted to be sitting at home with the man of my dreams before going to clean our teeth and snuggling up until the morning.

I was feeling lonely. Terribly lonely.

I had always imagined that, by that stage in life I'd be happily married and living in a lovely little house in the country with a couple of beautiful, healthy children playing in the garden. And, of course, a couple of horses in the field behind the house.

But in my loneliest moments, I would have given up on my dream future, just to be able to share my life with someone. I was fed up of getting up on my own and going to bed on my own. I wanted someone with whom I could make some real plans for the future. Someone to go on holiday with. Someone to talk to.

I wanted to love and to be loved.

I had been in this place so many times before that I knew I could keep going, and I knew the depression would lift. And when it did, I knew I needed to do something positive. It was time for action; time to get my positive pants on! And so I made a decision:

Online dating! I would start online dating.

It wasn't an easy decision. I'd always imagined I'd meet someone special at work or through a mutual friend. And even though I knew so many people who were already doing it, I couldn't shake the sense that it was a little bit sad. (Don't forget, this was before the social acceptance of certain swipe-left-and-right apps.) Weren't all these people just a bunch of desperate losers?

The answer to that is no. For a start, I didn't see myself as a desperate loser, and there I was about to embark on online dating.

So, I went on my online adventure and stuck up a teeny tiny profile picture. (That bit made me feel terribly exposed.) I wrote up a bit of blurb about me. That was hard! I wanted to be honest about what I was looking for, but didn't want to sound either too keen or too flippant.

Publish.

There. It was done. Ali Douglas was dating again. Well, in a virtual sense.

It didn't take long to arrange my first date. I agreed to meet a rather hot-looking guy who professed to be into skiing and surfing. And I was very pleasantly surprised to see that he looked like his photo. I was also pleasantly surprised to learn that he was a very nice and non-weird kind of a guy. And that he really was into skiing and surfing.

But, much as he ticked lots of boxes on paper, there was no spark. Next!

As time went on, I realised that, in the main, the guys were genuine. Like me, they just hadn't met their soulmate yet, so they had turned to more modern ways of dating.

One guy said he reckoned his perfect woman was the hide-and-seek champion of the world! That amused me.

But, for all the good eggs out there, there were some absolute horror shows. One guy invited me to a very plush hotel bar in Central London and crassly ordered one of the most expensive bottles of champagne on the menu.

I was decidedly unimpressed with that sort of pretentious behaviour. Champagne was my tipple of choice, but he didn't know that. He was only interested in proving to me – and everyone else in the bar – that he was a man with money. He spoke loudly. His specialist subject was himself. And frankly, champagne aside, I found him to be conceited and arrogant. He was, without doubt, his own biggest fan.

I politely declined his champagne in favour of a plain old vodka and slim. The result of this, however, was that he quaffed the entire bottle of bubbles and got embarrassingly drunk. But then, horror of all horrors, he tried to make off without paying! I soon remedied that though. I frog-marched him back to the bar and the drivelling idiot had to cough up. Quite right too.

I did, however, agree to share a taxi home with him, since he was practically passing my flat. With hindsight I should probably have run a mile as soon as we left the hotel, but I had my practical head on and it just made sense to split the cost.

Hilariously though, he tried in his slurred and garbled way to tell the cab driver to go to his place first, then double back and drop me off. I'm Scottish. I knew his game. He was trying to lumber me with the cab fare. The barefaced cheek! Thankfully, the driver was all over his little game, and took me home first.

Then there was the guy with the flatulence problem ...

He took me to a lovely little restaurant in Chelsea then to a football match at Stamford Bridge.

Now, on first noticing the horrendous smell, I assumed it was from someone else. Who goes on a date and lets rip? Like, constantly? But by the time we were midway through the first half of the game, it became clear that the disgusting farmyard stench was coming from his bottom.

I'm not good at smells at the best of times. This, though, was on another level altogether.

I couldn't even stay until full-time. I was silently retching, and was in real danger of doing an actual chunder in Mr Abramovich's beautiful stadium.

I was getting pretty fed up with dating. I'd worked my way through countless guys over a period of more than a year. Despite some of them being interesting and decent, funny and kind, that wasn't enough. I wanted to meet "the one".

Sometimes one date was enough to know that there was no point in arranging date number two. Sometimes one date would lead to a few dates. But for whatever reason, none of them stood the test of time.

I remember quite clearly thinking I'd give it one more week, then knock it on the head and just accept that I was destined never to have a husband or children.

During that week, I resurrected my one-woman 'Operation TV' enterprise and reformatted it for dating! For those last few days, I dedicated every spare minute to that dating website! I scoured endless pages of strangers smiling out at me. I went through their profiles with a fine-toothed comb to make sure there was some common ground, and that I wasn't wasting either their time or mine. I got into numerous online conversations with a whole bunch of them.

After much whittling down, I set up lunch and dinner dates for every day the following week. It was going to be an expensive week, but I wanted to know that, if I was going to give this thing up, I'd given it my best shot.

By the Friday, I was not only feeling massively discouraged, but was also a couple of pounds heavier from all the eating out. Where was my man? My soulmate? He really was the-hide-and-seek champion, and I didn't want to play that game any more. I was fed up of looking.

I'd set Saturday as my final day of dating. That poor guy. Little did he know just how much was resting on that one little meeting!

Without knowing exactly where, we knew we lived close to each other in London. So, we chose a local coffee shop.

Two double skinny cappuccinos later and I knew my search was over. I knew I had just met my future husband.

CHAPTER 21

LIFE WITHOUT MEDS

Within 15 months of that final date, I was married and had a son.

I was living in a house in the country with, wait for it, my two beautiful horses in the field next to the house.

On the face of it, I had everything I had ever wanted.

Life can be challenging though, and sadly our marriage wasn't to last. A few short years later, we were divorced. It is as amicable as these things can be though, and our precious little boy, MK, was our gift from this time together.

*

Falling pregnant when you live with bipolar doesn't come without its challenges.

I was 38 when I fell pregnant. An older mum? Well yes, I guess so, but it's all relative, isn't it? I certainly didn't feel old. Still don't for that matter. But I was decidedly unimpressed when a nurse casually joked about me being a "geriatric mum".

A what?! Apparently, that was how they used to describe pregnant women over the age of 35. How lovely! I believe the term nowadays, and it's still hugely unflattering, is: "women of advanced maternal age". Again, lovely!

Of all the challenges of being a pregnant woman with bipolar, the toughest thing of all, for me anyway, was dealing with my meds. Or rather, the lack of them.

All those hateful, yet at the same time, wonderful meds that I was taking every day, had to stop. They had to be fully out of my system for at least three months before I fell pregnant.

There have been times when I have resented taking them. The side effects can be pretty grim … but I resented not taking them far more.

No antidepressant? No mood stabiliser? Seriously?!

The prospect of slowly reducing my intake filled me with creeping dread. (Imagine watching a gruesome horror movie, on your own, with the lights switched off, sinister music at full blast – oh and for good measure, let's say, you're in a haunted house, in the middle of a very dark forest.) That bad. No exaggeration.

The withdrawal from citalopram was particularly miserable. Being on the maximum dose meant that to deprive myself of such a hefty quantity of chemicals was quite a shock to the system, with such lovely symptoms as:

- Anxiety.
- Serious dizziness. Constantly.
- The concentration of a two-year-old in an astrophysics lecture.
- Confusion over simple things like organising my journey into work.
- Crying until I ran out of tears.
- Low mood. Very low mood.
- Mental and physical exhaustion.
- Headaches.
- Irritability.
- Being unable to complete a sentence without losing my train of thought halfway through it.
- Senior moments. Although of course, these may have been more down to the fact that I was a geriatric. Losing my phone, then finding it in the fridge or the linen basket wasn't uncommon.

Nonetheless, if I was hoping to fall pregnant, that was the way it had to be. Happily, I got pregnant very quickly after stopping the meds, but still had to stay chemical-free to protect the soon-to-be-born little MK.

My pregnancy was quite an ordeal.

Bipolar aside, I was hungrier than a bear after a winter of hibernation. I ate for 102 as opposed to just two, but maybe that's not terribly unusual for a lot of pregnant women.

I developed a weird disorder called Symphysis Pubis Dysfunction, which made walking so difficult that the doctor offered me the use of a wheelchair until MK was born. I opted for crutches instead.

And as for the symptoms of my mental illness? They didn't disappoint. Without the powerful presence of my meds to keep them at bay, they had free rein to cause havoc.

I withdrew from friends, and to a lesser but still significant degree, from family.

I was bad tempered and snappy.

I felt horribly low and lost.

I cried incessantly.

I was scared. Really scared.

I felt as though I'd lost something but had absolutely no idea when or where I'd last had it. I was aimless.

My mood swings were so severe that I went back to my GP. She was fantastic; she had a solid understanding of mental health, and given my track record, wasted no time in referring me for specialist help with a new psychiatrist.

The psychiatrist suggested that, as I had passed the three-month mark in my pregnancy, I could go back on a lower dose of some of my meds. I was terrified of doing anything to harm the miraculous, tiny little MK growing inside me. He was entirely dependent on me making good decisions for both of us, and I'd already fallen madly and deeply in love with him. But the doctor reassured me that because all his organs were now formed, the risks of harming MK were now very low, and that the benefits far outweighed the risks.

The bottom line was, I had to take some kind of action. I was carrying the horrible fear that if I didn't get myself back on an even keel, I wouldn't be allowed to keep my little MK. I had convinced myself that he'd be whisked away from me as soon as he was born.

Being back on the meds improved my mental wellbeing enormously. And just before Christmas 2012, my beautiful little MK made his entrance. Contrary to my belief that he would be torn away from me, he remained in my arms, and has barely left my side since.

That short spell of living without those life-changing drugs was an eye-opener though. A stark reminder of the old days.

That all too familiar feeling of being out of control came flooding back. The pandemonium in my mind. The tears. The complete lack of motivation. The inability to communicate. The isolation. The deep, gut-wrenching sadness.

It was a reminder of how lucky I'd been to have received an accurate diagnosis, and subsequently, the appropriate medication and support I needed. It was a reminder of how much I needed these drugs.

But, traumatic as it had been to relive those feelings from the past, it was all worth it. The day MK was born, he brought me a reason to be the best person I could be. To fight for emotional balance and to fight through the darkest of depressions.

Thank you MK. Thank you for being my superhero and my saviour.

CHAPTER 22

A BRAVE NEW WORLD

After the divorce, MK and I moved out of the family home and rented a tiny little barn conversion. It was very cute, but so "compact and bijoux" that in order to reach my bed, I had to close the bedroom door to clear enough space to bend myself around and onto the bed.

That was okay though. The stress of the breakup had resulted in my weight plummeting to under seven stone, so I could shimmy my way through that little gap with ease.

We had been spoilt for outside space in our previous house. Now MK's playground was nothing more than a small balcony. That was okay too, though. I would take MK to the park. And there were ducks at the park. We hadn't had ducks in the garden.

I had made the decision to take my life forward in this way. I had chosen to walk away from a very comfortable, secure life. I had braced myself for a very different kind of future to that which I'd had during my marriage. His daddy was still very loving and hands-on, and took him at weekends. But from my perspective, it was me and MK against the world.

And we really did need each other; the year we spent in our little barn was tough. The gremlin was ever-present. And, as always, he had identified the tell-tale signs of my vulnerability before unleashing his hateful charms.

Over the years, I'd slowly been learning to fight this nasty little gremlin. I'd learnt to answer him back. But he was persistent. He'd had more comebacks than Liberace. That didn't make him a 'shoo-in' to win though. He knew all too well how to creep up from behind and pounce, like a leopard hunting his prey. But this time, I felt like he'd met his match. MK was my foil. He was my right-hand man. My silent assassin.

Knowing that my sole purpose was to create a good and fulfilling life for this little boy gave me a strength I never knew I had.

I was still working in football TV. I was presenting and reporting for the Premier League two days a week, so still had an income. It was a fairly good income for two days' work, but not enough to survive on. MK's daddy paid a sensible maintenance too, but the combined amount wasn't going to get us very far in the long term.

For the first time in my life, I had to turn to the government for financial help. I received a contribution towards my rent and council tax.

I was as mortified as I was grateful for this help. I was grateful because without it, I'd have been in dire straits. I was mortified because I'm a proud woman.

I had always supported myself, and having to admit to needing help, simply to survive, felt wholly uncomfortable. I was in that frustrating, yet all too recognisable, situation for many single parents – if I'd worked more hours, the cost of childcare would have wiped out any earnings. In fact, I would probably have been out of pocket.

The hardest change to adapt to though, and the thing that made my mood plummet, was the lack of grown-up conversation.

MK was such great company, but there was only so much discussion we could have about Lego. And an hour-long game of hide-and-seek in our tiny little barn could get wearing, especially as MK hadn't yet grasped the concept that you weren't supposed to hide in the same place every time.

The barn was in the same area as the old house, so I still had a few friends with children of the same age nearby. Even so, play dates with the little ones didn't appease the loneliness. I was still stuck with my own company every evening.

I could have done more to see friends. I could have invited them over for supper, negating the need for a babysitter. I could have done that. But then again, I couldn't.

One of the gremlin's nasty streaks sees him try to cut me off from the real world and barricade me away from reality. Seeing and interacting with people becomes just too daunting. Even when I crave company, I'm securely locked in my solitary shell unable to budge. There's a ball and chain around my ankles, and guess who has the key? Yep. And he hangs onto it until the time he decides to set me free.

I suffered badly from depression during that time. There were very few highs, but more than enough lows to go around.

Once MK was bathed and tucked up in bed, I would try to chill in front of the TV. To switch off my anxiety and guilt-ridden mind. I couldn't help thinking that once again, I had caused hurt by breaking up the family unit. Irrespective of whether my decisions were the right ones or not, they had caused devastating hurt and upset.

Perhaps quite deservedly, managing to chill out was nigh on impossible for me. I would pace. I would scan the room, taking in my surroundings and wondering what on earth the future held. I would clean. I would prepare MK's packed lunch as far as I could the night before, ready for him to take to pre-school the following day.

I was going through a lot with the family at the time. Or rather, the family were going through a lot with me.

My poor parents were once again racked with worry over daughter number two. They had been so happy when I'd settled down and had little MK, yet there I was, back on uncharted territory, with absolutely no security or stability whatsoever.

Their worry spilled into upset. And at times, into anger. Understandably.

Initially, they questioned whether my decision-making over the divorce was a symptom of my illness. In fact, that point was raised on more than one occasion. But that frustrated me. I knew it wasn't connected with my illness. It was simply that I had fallen out of love, but I could absolutely understand why they were asking those questions. They were looking in from the outside, trying to make sense of my thinking. They were trying to understand what had made me choose this insecure existence. Again.

It was all very difficult.

The other battle I had was with my weight. Initially I lost weight without trying to. It was just a side effect of my tumultuous situation. But it soon escalated and became a conscious thing. I grew to like the feeling of losing weight, and felt a sense of satisfaction in knowing this was one area of my life that I could control.

I nibbled on peanuts and oatcakes during the day, but even they were strictly rationed.

And then, I began to make myself sick.

I couldn't bear the feeling of having anything in my stomach, and craved the "high" of feeling my stomach rumble as it cried out for nutrition.

There was one occasion when I went out for a Thai meal with a couple of friends. Knowing that I'd need to eat something more than a peanut sent me into a state of panic.

I dealt with it though. After my starter, I excused myself to nip off to the loo where I made myself sick. After my main course, I did the same. I had found the actual process of making myself sick really hard at first, but soon it became easy, and took no time at all. I had all the symptoms of bulimia, but I was too scared to take another problem to my GP.

Bulimia is such a complex illness. And it takes you to such a sad and lonely place where everything is secretive. I feel so much for those suffering with it.

I thought I looked better for having lost so much weight, although when I looked in the mirror, I would still see certain areas where I could afford to shrink a little more.

When I was invited to a swanky awards ceremony, I had to search high and low to find a size six dress to wear. (Even then it was a little loose on me.) It was only at that point that people really began to notice how far I had taken my obsession. It wasn't surprising. When I look back at the photos, even I think I look gaunt. My legs and arms hadn't an ounce of fat on them; I looked frail. And I had an empty smile, there was nothing of any conviction behind my eyes.

In the past, my weight obsession had been linked with my mood fluctuations, but in this case, I think it was down to a combination of things. Although I was depressed, I wasn't anything like as low as I had been prior to being diagnosed with my illness. It wasn't as though I felt so completely and utterly worthless that I didn't feel worthy of food.

Perhaps it was partially down to the fact that I felt insecure and vulnerable at being on my own again. Although this may sound terribly vain, I wanted to feel attractive. Emotionally I was a mess, but outwardly, I was desperate to appear capable of looking after myself and MK. And that meant, amongst other things, looking after my appearance.

This wholly unhealthy obsession lasted for around six or seven months before I finally regained control. Control, this time, of my health, as opposed to my need to avoid food. Once again, it was something I addressed myself. I gradually began to eat a little more, and to keep it down, and as the weeks and months rolled by, I eventually reached something resembling a healthy weight again.

I think the catalyst for forcing myself to get better was twofold.

Firstly, so many people were commenting on how much weight I'd lost. There were pictures of the awards ceremony, but they didn't want to speak to me about my dress or the ceremony itself. Almost without exception, the comments were on how skinny I had become.

At first, I found that strangely empowering. I felt as though I was succeeding at something. But there came a time when close friends were quietly telling me that I was taking it too far; they were worried about me.

I hated hearing that. I was upsetting the people who mattered most to me. Deep down I knew that, no matter how hard it would be to begin eating and put on a few pounds, it was in my power to do it. I had the ability to stop my friends from worrying.

Equal to that though, was my precious MK ... How could I sit with him at mealtimes and bang on about how he had to eat "one more mouthful" when I was struggling to hold down a single peanut?

Forcing myself to eat was like torture at first. I felt full up, two bites into my meal, and forcing myself to go on eating just made me feel sick.

Resisting the urge to make myself sick after every meal was tough. Really tough. And at first, I didn't always win that mental battle, but in time, and with great effort, I was able to eat a proper meal and keep it down.

As for stepping onto the scales though? That was crippling. Watching the numbers on the digital scales go up felt all wrong. At first, I felt as though all my "good work" had gone out of the window. But of course, what had practically been a starvation diet, was far from "good work".

Even now, I'm not completely clear of my unhealthy attitude to food. It's been hovering around at times throughout my life, and is something I still need to monitor. At least now I'm aware of its existence though, so I'm in the best position to make sure I don't drift off course again.

Standing in the face of all the challenges I faced during that time, there was always MK. He saved me from ever sinking into such deep depression that I wanted to end it all. And I fought my hardest to do my best for him.

His world had been turned upside down too. So, throughout it all, his daddy and I focused solely on helping him to settle into a new way of living – at Mummy's house during the week, and Daddy's house at the weekend. It sounds simple, but it was a massive upheaval for his little mind to process. MK was an absolute hero. He took it all in his stride, and I answered his inevitable questions as honestly as I could. He's a confident and secure little soul now, and we're all so proud of him.

On some level, I knew we'd be fine. I'd always been a fighter and a survivor, and with my precious MK in tow, I had more ammunition than ever to win whatever battles lay ahead.

As it turned out though – and what I couldn't possibly have known at the time – was that my future was going to lie in some unexpected directions ...

CHAPTER 23

IRRITATING PROD

It wasn't all bad when we lived at the barn. The time I spent in my own company was, I now believe, good for me. Yes, it was lonely for much of the time, and yes, I was dealing with a whole raft of emotions, but it gave me time to think. To reflect.

That said, the running theme was that, quite simply, bipolar sucks. It seriously sucks.

Even when I'm in a good, stable place, there's still a darkness on my radar. Makes sense; I'm clinically bipolar. It never totally disappears.

Everyone living with bipolar is battling, like Mel Gibson in *Braveheart*, with their painted faces and big shields to ward off their own gremlins.

Yet, despite having had some utterly horrendous episodes throughout the years – including that one particularly close call – my time of reflection made me realise that I'm actually a "glass half-full" kind of a girl.

Sounds weird, and almost doesn't ring true, I know. But it is true.

You know as well as anyone now, that I haven't always had this outlook. The meds and therapy had a profound effect on the way I processed things. And so did my family.

My parents are, without doubt, the most inspirational and positive pair of pensioners I know. They've experienced total devastation at times, and yet they always manage to retain the remarkable ability to create, to feel, and to spread joy.

To view that glass in an optimistic light again.

To accept.

Sometimes it's taken them longer than others, but that's okay, isn't it? It's okay to lick the agonisingly deep wounds that life can inflict, and to take as much time as you need to let them heal. Rushing the process is a bit like sticking a plaster on a broken leg, when only a cast will help it mend.

Time and patience are so hard to call on at times, but they're crucial to long-lasting mental health.

Oh my days, though! It took many years for me to reach that level of understanding.

Prior to my diagnosis and treatment, my glass was so empty that even the drips at the bottom of the glass had evaporated into thin air. I would have put two fingers up to anyone who said they had a "glass half-full" outlook yet professed to be living with bipolar.

But that time of enforced reflection in the barn also made me realise that I've come to accept that the lows will pass.

It's not a magic cure. It doesn't take away from the agonising sadness and despair that comes with a depressive episode. It doesn't stop me from hiding out for days, hugging my knees for comfort while silently wailing.

Nor does it make me feel optimistic at the time. Not right in the heat of the battle. If it was as good as that, I'd bottle it and dish it out to every battling soul on a free prescription.

So, what does it do then?

It comforts me. It keeps poking me in the arm to remind me the pain will pass. Not unlike little MK, when he's pleading for a chocolate digestive before tea. That persistent, irritating little prod.

The most welcome irritation ever.

Even when I brush the prod away, it must somehow seep into my subconscious. I know it must, or the overwhelming feelings of hopelessness and despair would remain – and they would destroy me.

Is it a learned behaviour? Hard to say. Is it nature versus nurture? Is it years of intensive therapy? Who knows.

What I do know, though, is that it keeps me afloat. And it helps me remember that we're all beautiful, unique and complex characters with our own ways of surviving the hell that our mental illness may lob at us.

That little prod isn't a crystal ball. It's yet to master the art of predicting the future. If it had been able to share its vision for my future, I'd have leapt out of my low mood with more bounce than the overexuberant Tigger from *Winnie-the-Pooh*.

I'd have thought it "ridickerus," as Tigger would say.

Utterly "ridickerus".

CHAPTER 24

TIMING IS EVERYTHING

Available: A washed-up, 42-year-old, divorced TV presenter and single mummy with serious mental health issues and no money.

There's an ad you don't see every day. But yep! That was me. Hardly the stuff that dreams are made of ...

So there we were, little MK and I, living our life, as best we could in our cutesy little barn. We'd settled into a routine. Looking back on it, it was a precious time. We bonded more than ever. We were a team.

MK was at pre-school for a few hours a day during the week. He had a weekly swimming lesson, the odd horse riding lesson (too expensive to be a regular thing), and a few play dates in between.

I would work on Thursdays and Fridays, while little MK went to his childminder. He loved his time there.

He spent weekends with his daddy, the result of which was that I loathed coming back from work on a Friday. Coming back to an empty house, and invariably, an empty weekend.

Saturday mornings were the worst time. I'd get up to deafening silence and go to bed in that same silence.

I'd watch Saturday morning cookery shows. I'd take my car to be washed. I'd clean. I'd iron. (I never iron.) But it took up some time.

Oh, and I'd cry. Standard. I'd cry lots. Hardly surprising. I was still trying to get over the divorce, the dramatic change in lifestyle, and the loneliness. And I was worried that I didn't know what our next steps would be. Living with that kind of uncertainty was hard. I'm a planner, and I didn't have a plan in place for our future.

And yet, I did still feel like things would work out.

On Sunday afternoon, MK would come back to the barn full of stories about what he'd got up to over the weekend. That was the best bit of the whole week. He was like a little shot of joy.

We'd play, and chat, before sitting down to a banquet of pesto pasta with sprinkles on top (grated cheese). The boy would have it for breakfast, lunch and dinner given half a chance. It was the feast of kings as far as he was concerned.

Our life would have gone on like that indefinitely had it not happened. But it did happen. And it was to change our lives forever.

Let's backtrack a few months ...

I was invited to a social event – and that's when a mutual friend introduced me to him ... That's when I first met Handsome Doc.

The event was held in the village where my ex-husband and I were still living. It was the last time he and I ever went out as a couple – our marriage was all but over by then, and we were starting to talk about divorce

Nonetheless, we had committed to this event ...

It was a race night held in one of the bigger houses in the village. A lot of work had gone into making the evening a success – there were fairy lights all the way up the driveway, which led into a horsebox! The horsebox itself was kitted out with a full-size model racehorse, and various other horsey items. As you walked down the ramp and out of the other side of the horsebox, the lights led you into the house where there was a champagne reception before the racing got underway.

Various horse races were shown on a big screen and the bets were no more than a couple of pounds each. It was just a bit of fun, and an excuse for a get-together.

I remember leaving my house that evening clutching my torch – there were no street lights in this tiny little hamlet. In fact, it consisted of only around 30 houses and a very pretty little twelfth-century church.

Mum had come down from Glasgow to visit and was looking after MK.

As we made our way along the pitch-black lane, we bumped into another couple, also going to race night. With them, was a tall and extremely handsome friend of theirs.

This was the first time I set eyes on Handsome Doc.

We spoke a bit during the course of the evening, but although there was an undeniable spark between us, the timing was every shade of wrong, so we went our own ways at the end of the night and that was that.

Or so we thought.

Months went by.

I did think about him from time to time, and would wonder what might have developed had we met at a different time.

Actually, to say that I thought about him "from time to time" might be me playing it a teeny bit cool. I thought about him a lot.

It just made me sad though. We had met at the wrong time in our lives and our paths were unlikely ever to cross again. But then came the text. I had, it seemed, popped into Handsome Doc's thoughts from time to time too. He knew I was now single, and wondered whether I'd like to meet for a drink.

I'm sure the relationship rulebook would say that I probably shouldn't have even considered getting involved with anyone so soon after the recent changes in my life. (And in fact, he probably shouldn't have considered it either.)

A drink though ... A drink was surely okay.

The drink went well. As did the dinner date to follow. As did the date at the rugby. As did the night out at a club that he'd recently joined in London.

Handsome Doc and I were nuts on each other.

Emotionally I felt well. Falling in love agreed with me.

Bipolar? Do one.

There was no way I was going to let the gremlin ruin this. I don't even think he could have. This was so much stronger. We felt unbreakable.

I told Handsome Doc that I lived with bipolar very early on in our relationship. It felt like the right thing to do. But I was nervous. Because he was a doctor, and had the "advantage" of knowing about the illness, that might have given him some serious reservations about dating someone affected by it.

But his reaction was, as I should have known, amazing.

We talked for hours the night that I opened up to him. I shared a lot about the journey which had brought me to that point in my life. He asked a lot of questions. And I didn't hold back with the answers. I didn't sugar-coat it. I didn't play it down. I said it all exactly as it was.

His reaction?

He told me it didn't scare him. He even thanked me for sharing something that must have taken a lot of courage to speak about.

That conversation took our relationship up a notch. I still felt nervous. I knew the dark times would come again. So too would the highs. And I knew that seeing those things in reality might put a different slant on things. I could only wait and hope …

And then, sure enough, a few months in, I did hit a low. But rather than lace up his running shoes and run for the hills, Handsome Doc was there for me. He was everything that I could have hoped he would be.

He didn't try to analyse what was going on for me. He didn't try to put it right. He simply asked what he could do to help.

I explained that I found it difficult to talk about my feelings in the midst of these episodes, but that I'd do my best to shed some light on it once the darkness had lifted.

In the meantime, I just needed his presence and his hugs. I always knew he was there for me, waiting to kiss my forehead and wipe away my tears.

He'd seen all my flaws and broken pieces, yet he loved me, and accepted me, exactly as I was; and still loves me exactly as I am.

It became clear that what Handsome Doc and I had was something special. Something different from anything either of us had experienced before.

Six months later, we bought a house and moved in together.

It was the start of the life I had always dreamt of. The start of a life with meaning; a life that would no longer be governed by mental illness.

PART IV
PRESENT DAY

CHAPTER 25

INDISCRIMINATE BIPOLAR

It's just over a year since we moved into our home in Surrey.

I love it. We love it.

The bond that has formed between my two boys is beautiful. Handsome Doc takes MK out on his bike. He plays football with him. We take it in turns to read him his bedtime story. MK gets so excited when he hears Handsome Doc arriving home from work, and the two of them can often be found sitting together on the sofa watching *Paddington!*

It warms my heart when I discover them sitting together, laughing and talking. Precious times.

The house itself feels warm and inviting (and it's a good party space too as we discovered when we had our house-warming).

It's a happy home.

It's happy because we're happy. It's warm and inviting for the same reason. But also because Handsome Doc and I spent several months creating our perfect little sanctuary. I absolutely love designing interiors. It's a real passion of mine.

The colour scheme throughout the house is simple. It's predominantly varying shades of grey, punctuated with some black and cream. There are outsized sofas and armchairs. There are lots of floor plants, which we've lit with mini concealed uplighters.

There are always flowers on the dining table and the breakfast bar thanks to the most wonderful birthday gift from Handsome Doc of a delivery of fresh flowers every week. Lilies are my favourite. They're so vibrant and clean-looking.

The house is open plan with big windows and bi-folding doors, meaning that it's always filled with light, which is important for me. Being in a dull space lowers my mood.

The bedroom has double doors leading out into the garden, and when it's warm, we leave them open at night, which I love. It almost feels as though we're sleeping outside.

The house has lots of photos of friends and family on the walls. I still sometimes pause as I'm passing a photo to look at the familiar faces smiling out at me. I find them so evocative. They capture a particular moment in time when I can clearly remember the way I was feeling. The music that was playing. The conversations we were having, and the joy we felt.

Every family member and close friend is represented, including my gorgeous grandparents from both sides, who have all passed away now. I'll always love and miss them.

MK's *Paw Patrol* decorated room doesn't adhere to the rules of the house. One feature wall is painted bright turquoise, which is one of the colours on the *Paw Patrol* curtains and bedding. I can't stand it! But it's right for him. He loves it, and that's what matters.

It's his space. His little bolthole where he can make the rules. He can tip up his enormous great toy chest and scatter everything all over the floor if he wants too. There's only one boss in that room, and it's not me.

Ordinarily, I don't like having clutter lying around. It makes me anxious. I can't expect MK to respect my OCD boundaries though, and funnily enough, I don't have any problem with him pulling out every toy he owns. Even in the main living area. In fact, I encourage it. I want him to be able to play wherever he wants to, and if that's downstairs with us, so much the better.

But! When he goes to bed I clear it all away, out of sight. Those Lego pieces are a nightmare to find, and I always manage to stand on one in my bare feet. Painful!

Clearing his toys away is a military process. They don't just get lobbed in anywhere with gay abandon, they're neatly stored in their dedicated cupboard.

Not long before we moved to our happy home, I handed in my notice at work to become a full-time mummy and homemaker. It was a funny feeling. Like many of us, work had been a huge feature in my life. I had always enjoyed earning my own money, and relished the satisfaction of a successful day in the studio.

But, stopping work was a decision we reached for two reasons. Firstly, I hadn't really been enjoying the job I had been doing latterly. I was still working for the Premier League, which was a lovely company to work for and I had a fantastic boss, but I was reporting more often than presenting, and never felt comfortable with that.

Given that I had always been a studio presenter, I didn't feel polished as a reporter. I felt out of my comfort zone, which isn't conducive to live TV, where the viewer needs to feel confident that you know what you're doing. As we know from previous experience!

I thrived on doing live TV in the studio. I loved the buzz I felt when I saw the on-air light and felt the adrenaline rush; knowing that there was no going back; that this was being beamed to the nation. And on that channel, worldwide.

There was no room for error. Although there was a certain satisfaction in improvising solutions when things went wrong. Knowing that, if there was a problem with the live feed to a reporter, I could cope with it. I had the confidence to know that I could take the programme forward by ad-libbing.

I also loved interviewing studio guests. I enjoyed asking questions which made the guest think, and hopefully, asking the questions that the viewers wanted me to ask. It's quite a responsibility. Especially as you're putting yourself out there to be knocked down.

It's an unforgiving industry. If someone behind the scenes cocks up, they're not the ones who have to face the music on screen. It falls to the presenter to deal with the mistake. And it's the presenter who's judged on how they deal with the mistake. Nobody is going to know that it was actually the director or the vision mixer who messed up.

But after more than 20 years of presenting, I began to lose my passion for it. When that happens, it comes across on air. It isn't a job you can do well unless you absolutely love it.

I wanted to make the decision to leave the business, rather than have the business make the decision for me.

Aside from my job, Handsome Doc and I were acutely aware that little MK had gone through yet more upheaval when we had all moved in together. As ever, the little fellow has taken it all in his stride, but that doesn't take away from the fact that he has experienced a heck of a lot of change in his young life.

I want to be there for him. To create stability for him. To give him a routine. I want him to know that Mummy will always be at the school gate to greet him after school, with a big smile and a hug. Being at home throughout the week means I can do that.

Day-to-day life is good. Really good. Little MK is flourishing in every way. He loves school and seems really happy at home too. He knows his routine of being with us during the week and with his daddy at the weekend. It works.

And Handsome Doc and I are deliriously happy ...

Bipolar?

Ah yes, that's the only fly in the ointment.

The three of us have had to open the doors of our home to my illness too. The good news, though, is that Handsome Doc has seen the way it affects me on every level, and is still here.

He's seen the highs. He's seen the lows. But happily, he's seen plenty of the in-between times too when I'm just me.

To the outside world I live a privileged life. I've found love in a way that I never knew existed. I live in a beautiful little house in a safe neighbourhood, and I've been blessed with a wonderful son who brings me enormous joy every single day of my life.

I have no money worries. We go on lovely holidays. And I have wonderful, supportive friends and family.

So how can I possibly live with a mental illness? What kind of ungrateful, self-absorbed person can feel sorry for themselves with a life like this?

A person like me. I can.

And that's the thing with bipolar. It's irrelevant how good life may appear to be. This illness doesn't single out the sad and the lonely. It doesn't just descend on the weak or the vulnerable. It's indiscriminate. It has no care for who it chooses to inflict itself upon.

Let's look at the facts.

I'm the girl who hums happy tunes, even when I'm pushing my wonky trolley around the supermarket. I "do coffee" and ladies' lunches. Well, I say "lady", but I may be slightly flattering myself there. Or at least, Handsome Doc would raise an eyebrow.

I laugh. I'm occasionally funny. Well, mildly amusing. Another raised eyebrow from Handsome Doc.

I walk tall (despite being just 5ft 3in).

I smile and chat with the school lollipop lady. I even high fived the school caretaker when I walked MK through the school gate last week. On reflection, that really wasn't cool. He high fives every child as they skip through the gates in the morning. He does not, I repeat, not, high five the parents. Ever. I'm sorry Mr Caretaker. My bad.

So how can this seemingly "normal," carefree and capable mummy have a mental illness, which at times makes her feel depressed?

She just can.

Not so long ago I had a low that lasted for three days. Bleurgh!

Now, we mustn't confuse it with the times before I was diagnosed, when the lows lasted for weeks and came with ideations of suicide. It still hit me pretty badly though ...

When the doorbell rang, I fled into the bedroom like a stealth bomber and stopped breathing until the coast was once again clear. Phew! That was close.

'I'm sorry, neighbour,' (at least I think it was you at the door), 'but do call again in a few days and I promise you I'll run towards the door, not away from it.'

Then, when I took MK to school, I disguised my pyjamas (rather stylishly, I'd like to think), with Ugg boots, a puffy jacket and beanie hat. Well I had to, didn't I? Firstly, I wanted to be invisible, but also, it shaved off a good 15 seconds when it came to collapsing back into bed when I got back home at 9.00am. The bed, which I stayed in for three solid days, bar a few trips to the fridge for yet another 1.75l bottle of Coke Zero, some trips to the loo (which were frequent due to the excessive consumption of said Coke Zero), and of course the school runs.

My hair was crying out to be washed to the point where I'm convinced there were various species of wildlife nesting in there. Showering? Are you serious? Not happening. Not today, not the next day, and most definitely not the next.

Tears? Oh, my goodness, were there tears? That desperate sadness had enveloped my very being once again.

But guess what? It passed. It passed as it always does, and I became me again.

This big low – as often happened – was preceded by an even bigger high. And, as ever, high-as-a-kite Ali was very interesting company ... it wasn't so much that I exchanged pleasantries with the lollipop lady, more that I had to quash the urge to hug her and swing her round, telling her how much she suited fluorescent yellow. Oh, and how well she wore her lollipop.

How she carried it and moved it with such effortless grace and finesse.

I'm hugely relieved and proud that I managed to supress that urge. It was a close call though. Could've been very embarrassing.

And then when poor Handsome Doc got home from work, after another long, tough day as a consultant anaesthetist – dealing with devastation and loss – on an almost daily basis, he got me talking at him for three hours straight. Just what he needed

But my 3D plan for landscaping the garden just had to be explained in agonising detail right there and then. The new range of black garden furniture I'd sourced online would offset the raised flower beds, all of which would be filled with just white flowering shrubs. And as for the Pieris japonica 'Sarabande'? It favours shade. Ideal for our south-westerly facing garden. Who knew?

Poor Handsome Doc. He's my rock and my hero. His unwavering love and support during these challenging episodes is nothing short of incredible.

It was bipolar exemplified though. A case study to prove that no matter what you have or don't have in life, bipolar will still thrive.

At least, it'll try to.

CHAPTER 26

A GOOD DAY

The good days far outweigh the bad days now.

I believe that's partly because of my meds and therapy, partly because I've found happiness, and partly because getting through the bad times has meant that I've built a strength and resilience to fight the gremlin.

The good days make me reflect back on just how far I've come. Joy, energy, love, light and laughter. Oh, and optimism. Not a bad line-up of emotions, don't you think?

I don't know why some days are like that. I'm not even sure that it helps to analyse them. But I do know that any day when the hypomania stays quiet and the gremlin stays hidden is a precious day in a life blighted with bipolar. And one day in particular ...

No way was this going to be a duvet day; it had all the makings of a dynamic day. So, up with the lark, long before Handsome Doc and young MK.

Shower, and then, wait for it ... hair wash. And, at the risk of going too far, my fuzzy legs got the razor treatment too ... along with everything else that I like to keep smooth. Enough said on that though.

This wasn't a joggers and a hoody kind of a day. It was more about my vintage blue jeans; black, high-heeled, ankle-length sock boots; a black, long-sleeved T-shirt; and my black belt with the big, chunky, silver buckle.

I love the jeans. I got them fairly recently and they're skinny on the thigh with a gradual bootcut flare. Definitely a bit vintage, but the best thing about them is that, when your heels are hidden under the bootcut, it looks as though you've had leg extensions!

Making an effort with my appearance is always a sign that I'm in a good place mentally.

Breakfast for MK when he surfaced, coffee for Handsome Doc, make-up and a bit of hair straightening action for me, then out the door for the school run. On time. I repeat: on time!

Smooth legs and smooth hair, how could the day get any better?

After the school run, it was home to meet the builder and greet him with a big hug for bringing over and fitting our new radiator cover. And yes, these things really do delight me. This was no show of hypomania. It was genuine excitement over a handmade radiator cover. (I should just say that the builder has spent several months working in the house, so I do actually know him quite well. He even knows about my bipolar.)

In stepped the neighbours. The mummies in our lane are tight. Bearing in mind we're new to the neighbourhood, I've become pretty close to them too. They're real and kind. We're way beyond the whole borrowing a cup of sugar thing. On that particular day, our chat ranged from laser hair removal to me peeing into a cup in the car. (I'll leave that one there if it's all the same to you).

There was a routine visit to the supermarket and another school pickup, then MK's football session, where I stood next to a very chatty mum. And, as she chatted, I wondered whether she was fighting her own battle? Maybe, just maybe, she really needed to chat? Maybe our seemingly inconsequential exchange was her saving grace for that day? I'm glad we spoke. I think it helped us both in different ways.

Home with a hungry MK, then the doorbell heralded a mad burst of activity. The chihuahua almost bust a gut trying to get to the door. MK tried to beat him to it. In the end it was a photo finish. It was another one of our neighbours and her two little boys, dropping off pressies for us from her recent holiday.

This really was a good day!

The arrival of Handsome Doc from work had the usual impact – it made me (and MK) silly happy.

That day gave me everything I craved: pure, uncomplicated freedom of spirit. Nothing too taxing, just me being at peace with myself and the world.

There was no reckless behaviour. There was moderation. There was balance. There was purity.

At no point was I in danger of going on some hypomanic-created drug- or alcohol-fuelled bender. Or looking for a false high.

At no point did I pace the house (at top speed) inventing completely unnecessary tasks to keep me busy and create imaginary perfection. There was perfect imperfection.

There were good decisions. There were contentment, gratitude and a beautiful, unassuming inner peace.

On that day, my illness had allowed me a good day.

When I look back over the years, I find it almost incomprehensible to accept that I now enjoy these days on a regular basis. They used to be so much rarer.

I'll never take them for granted though, nor will I ever let them pass without the recognition they deserve. I've battled hard for these days, and I don't ever intend to give them up without one almighty big fight.

CHAPTER 27

OPENING UP

In years gone by, I didn't divulge that I lived with bipolar. Not even to my closest friends. That meant that there was a huge part of my life we didn't share.

Looking back on it now, that saddens me. But the prospect of saying that I had to take pills to keep me sane (or almost sane), was unthinkable.

Surely my friends would think I was some kind of weirdo, and would distance themselves from me? And yet again, bipolar would have succeeded in alienating me from society.

It's incredible to think that I was afraid to admit to having bipolar, given that it's such a real and dangerous illness. But things are very different now.

My friends not only know about my illness; they understand and accept it. They understood and accepted immediately after I told them. I should have known that all along. These girls aren't my best friends in the world for no reason.

One close friend famously said that if I was a weather warning, I'd be "sunshine mixed with some sudden but severe hurricanes" and that people would be advised to stay indoors. Fair point. Weather warnings aside though, these girls rock. They heal my soul when it hurts, and squeeze my hand when I'm high.

This truly came to light when Handsome Doc and I hosted a house-warming party. The house looked fab, and I was so looking forward to seeing everyone. People started arriving at 8.00pm and the last of our guests left at 6.00am. It was a good party!

Had I been going to a party rather than hosting it, I would have felt anxious. This was different though. Even though there were around 60 people coming, they were all our friends.

There was dancing and lots of laughs. I paused for a moment at one point to take it all in and felt so blessed to have such a wonderful circle of friends They were all mixing so well. Many of them had never met, and it was lovely to see how they interacted. I'm sure there were some new friendships formed too, which warmed my heart.

As I look back on that evening, I feel happy that I was able to conduct myself in the way that I did. I felt relaxed and at ease. Comfortable in my own skin. I was at peace throughout the weekend.

It could have been the perfect situation for the gremlin to press the hypomanic button, which could have ruined everything. At times, I was teetering dangerously close to it, but I had made a plan to keep checking in on my mood, and it worked. Handsome Doc was keeping an eye on me too.

At times, I could feel my heart racing and my speech quickening. And then alarm bells started to ring when I was finding it difficult to concentrate on a conversation. (Clear signs that I need to take a breath and reset.)

A quick toilet trip for some deep breathing got me back on track, and in the right frame of mind to enjoy the party.

Enjoyment! That's something I used to find very difficult to master. Either I'd be hurtling along in a false sense of happiness, riding the wave of another high, or I'd be in the depths of despair, where manifesting anything resembling enjoyment is nigh-on impossible.

This was genuine enjoyment though. Oh, how life has changed!

The inevitable depressive low came in the early stages of the following week, just as I had dreaded. It's as though I've used up all my happy hormones, and as I wait for them to regenerate, the sad hormones rule the roost. Not a very medically correct description, but that's the way I view it.

This time, I didn't even try to fight. Instead, I just let my gremlin wreak his usual havoc and then jog on when he didn't get a reaction.

It was still awful. Tears, loneliness, deep sadness, utter exhaustion and total lack of communication were all present and correct, as usual. Plus, I missed my friends. Our time together was special, but it reminded me how far away we are geographically. Two of my oldest and dearest friends – Ruby who I've known since nursery and Jacqu from my printing company days – had travelled over 400 miles to come and join us for our house-warming. (Facetime is great, but no substitute for the real thing.)

What really hit home for me, though, was just how truly lucky I am to have such a supportive network to turn to. And how this support has deepened after me having told people about my illness.

My close friends are so in tune with me. I can't bear to think where I'd be without them.

Over the years we've partied, grieved, laughed and cried together. We've talked for hours on end. We've held hands through the dark times, and felt joy and happiness as we've grown, changed and, at times, achieved over the decades.

A couple of days after the party, Jacqu called me to ask if I was feeling better yet. I was confused and told her she was a genuine nutter – even more so than me – I said I'd never been poorly.

She simply said, 'I know you, Ali. Are you feeling better?'

Wow, she was good.

She'd suspected my mood would take a dip after the euphoria of the weekend. She also knows me well enough to know that I will never reach out in the middle of it, but will tell her about it afterwards.

I do this knowing that she, along with my other friends, are still standing alongside me metaphorically.

Ruby knows the signs too. She phone-stalks me when I go quiet and don't answer messages or calls.

They know. They just know.

They were in my life long before I was diagnosed with bipolar, long before I'd had any treatment or meds. They've seen the pain and heartache as I've gone through the blackest of times in my life, and they've seen the equally alarming euphoria, when, at times, they've found it hard to recognise me.

They've stood by me. They've had faith in me. They've held me up when I've needed it. These girls are rocks, and I know how lucky I am.

But the most important thing for me is that I've learnt the power of opening up about my illness. Contrary to my fears that it would alienate me, it's actually brought me closer than ever to my friends. It's given me an added strength.

Opening up is not an easy thing to do.

But in my experience, the prospect of opening up is actually far worse than the reality of doing so.

I've found that by learning to take ownership of who I am, and not feeling ashamed, I've had nothing but positivity in return.

I only wish I'd done it sooner.

CHAPTER 28

SHADES OF GREY

What was it that Dad said all those years ago?

'Everything you do, you do to extremes.'

Dad's right about most things, and that was no exception.

When I started blogging about my life with bipolar, I was really nervous about baring my soul. At first, I wrote a couple of blog posts which I ran past our friends, Mark and Shabana, and their feedback was so helpful. It forced me to think about what I was trying to get across and why.

I knew they'd be honest, and not afraid to tell me that certain bits were either irrelevant or could be misconstrued in some way. Then, I found a platform I liked, and duly set up my website. I didn't stop there though …

Cue the 'one-woman enterprise' all over again.

Blogging was the cornerstone of the project, but there were offshoots too. I wanted to reach out to as many people as I could in the hope that, by sharing my own experiences, I may be able to offer some form of comfort or support to others fighting their own battles.

I joined Twitter. Yes, I realise I'm a complete dinosaur for not having done it sooner, but I got there in the end.

I joined Instagram. As above!

I scoured both social media platforms to find people who were interested in mental health, so that I could share my blog posts and reach more people. I also wanted to read about other people's experiences of mental illness.

I earmarked all the big mental health charities, and contacted each one to ask if they'd be interested in publishing one of my blog posts on their website. Some, remarkably, said yes.

And then, lo and behold, I took it one step further and contacted a publisher to ask whether they'd be interested in publishing my book. A book that was yet unwritten, but was beginning to form in my mind. You already know what happened as a result of that.

I approached the whole thing in much the same way as I did my endeavours to break into television all these years ago. Only this time, it was different.

Yes, I obsessed. Yes, I spent every spare minute on it when MK was either asleep or at school.

But no, I never let it control me. I controlled it.

You know by now, that I'm not immune from hypomanic episodes, but the difference is that they come and go. And I know they don't tend to last for more than a day or so. That doesn't mean they can't still create all sorts of unexpected problems though ...

Last year I was in town at 11.00am on 11th November. The entire place ground to a halt as everybody observed a two-minute silence to commemorate the end of the First World War.

I paid my respects too, but if you've ever tried to stay still and quiet at the height of a hypomanic episode, you'll know it was a tall order.

I ended up screwing my eyes tightly shut and concentrating like mad on images of our brave servicemen and women who had given their lives for our freedom. I would always honour our war heroes, but it wouldn't always involve quite such an effort to keep still.

Thankfully, neither my feet, nor my mouth, moved. And in fact, not unusually for me, I became quietly emotional. Standard.

During the writing of this book I've experienced hypomania.

On the odd occasion I've stayed up all night, my thoughts running through my head so quickly that I've had to keep stopping what I'm doing to remind myself where I am, and what I'm doing. In fact, it's been more than the odd occasion, and Handsome Doc could see that it was getting out of control. With his help, I managed to keep more sensible hours. Note to self: I'm not a bat. I need to sleep at night, and be on form for MK during the day.

You know that "glass half-full" thing though? Well, in this case it applied to the speed of my typing. During hypomanic episodes, I can tap away on my laptop like an Olympic touch typist. With my words-per-minute count, I could write a trilogy of books in one night.

Towards the end of writing this book, my anxiety ramped up and I didn't sleep for around 60 hours. I barely even stopped for 60 seconds.

For that three-day period, I almost reverted back to ways of old. Almost, but not quite.

The house was cleaned and polished to within an inch of its life, but this time, I didn't dig out the nail brush to clean the carpets. I polished our big, beautiful, oak coffee table so much that it's now half the thickness it once was. I didn't get the sander out to smooth out the grain and rewax it though.

The washing machine wasn't off long enough for the drum to stop spinning from the last cycle, before it was ordered into action yet again.

I played tennis (badly) on the second day of this episode, but with the drive and energy of Federer a point away from clinching the Grand Slam. Sadly, I didn't play with anything like his talent.

I mapped out my diary for the next six months, all in my best handwriting, and in pencil, so that I could rub it out if my plans changed. (And still keep it looking neat.)

Surprising as it may seem though, my beautiful little MK saw his mummy at her best on these days. I had energy to burn and so did he, so why not join forces until our collective energy eventually burned out? It meant he got a bonus bike ride before supper, and even more activity crammed into his day. It certainly felt like the best way to manage all that hypomanic energy.

In the midst of that high, because it lasted longer than is now the norm, I was willing it to come to an end. Just so that my weary body and mind could rest. And my fingers! They were practically red raw from all the typing.

I knew, of course, that the end of the high would signal the start of a low. That's just how you live when you have bipolar, and it means I constantly have my foot on the brakes in a bid to slow down. I still go at quite a tilt, but I'm not on the same sort of rampage I once was. My life, like the colour scheme in my house, has come to incorporate a lot more shades of grey.

I will always loathe and detest the gremlin for imposing himself on me and my loved ones, and I still dread his presence. But I'm better armed than I used to be, and he doesn't scare me anymore.

CHAPTER 29

HAVE I BEEN TOO GENEROUS?

I have a rational head now. At least, for the most part. I try to resolve my worries and concerns by bringing them into the open and talking them through.

There is one thing that plays on my mind heavily though ...

Have I put my precious MK at risk?

There's been so much research into the cause of bipolar, but as yet, no one really knows where it stems from. Some people suspect it's caused by a chemical imbalance in the brain. More and more though, it's thought that there's a genetic link. That you are more likely to develop bipolar if a close family member has the condition.

So where does that leave my little MK? Could this mean that he's going to have to battle with his mind every single day in the same way that I, and so many others, do?

I watch over the moods of this incredible little creature more closely than he watches *Boss Baby*.

I am the person who is meant to protect this kind, innocent, and loving little boy from danger – and yet I might also be the person who has put him at risk.

There's a really hard balance to strike in observing his moods. (Funny that: I have bipolar. Balance isn't a word that is immediately associated with me.) The difficulty is that, while I do want to keep an eye on him, I don't want to start seeing symptoms of bipolar that aren't there.

His mood can flip more quickly than Mark Foster can do a flip turn in the swimming pool. One minute we're howling with laughter as he zips down the lane in his little electric car, then the next he can be breaking his heart and feeling angry and frustrated, when he decides the horn on his little black car isn't as loud as the one in my car.

His world has just ended. His car is rubbish. He hates it. He storms out of it and is "never going in it again".

Like mummy like son. Puts me in mind of my driving lessons with Dad.

That's normal five-year-old behaviour though, isn't it? At least I think it is. I hope it is. I'm sure it is.

I want to allow him to be himself and not to overanalyse everything. But I worry.

Five-year-olds are meant to suddenly leap off the sofa to run wildly around the house, entirely out of control, oblivious to their surroundings, and making more noise than a room full of trombonists. Aren't they?

Yes, of course they are.

He's a perfectly normal five-year-old, displaying perfectly normal five-year-old behaviour. It's normal for children to feel down, irritable, angry, hyperactive or rebellious at times.

He's still a baby. It's hard enough for us adults to make sense of our emotions, let alone fearless little boys like MK. And he should be given free rein to be that little boy. To explore his emotions. To switch from being deliriously happy one minute to being inconsolably upset the next.

It's normal. I know that.

And the reality is that, although bipolar can occur at any age, it's most often diagnosed in older children and teenagers. That said, in my case, the symptoms were there from a very early age.

But if this genetic link is true, how come I have bipolar? No one else had it before me.

Or maybe they did. It's always possible that it was present and went undiagnosed. I think that may well have been the case actually, but I'll never know. Mental illness was such a taboo subject with the generations before me, meaning that very few people sought help.

My grandparents' generation had endured at least one world war, and from what I understand, going to the doctor with a fluctuation in mood would have seemed self-indulgent, given the loss of life and the cruelty that they had witnessed.

Of course, it would not have been self-indulgent. But I do understand the overwhelming impulse to keep it under wraps.

I guess it doesn't really matter where my illness came from.

But where MK is concerned, the statistics speak for themselves. There is almost certainly a genetic link, and little MK has a greater chance of having bipolar than he would if his mummy didn't have it.

Perhaps I can steer him in the direction of safety by providing stability, love and conversation? Or am I being unrealistic? An imbalance is an imbalance.

Every time my brain spirals out of control and tries to convince me otherwise, I remind myself that he's got more chance of being well than of not being well.

The actual risk that a child with a parent who has the diagnosis will go on to develop it, is put at about 10 to 15 per cent. On first discovering that, I panicked. That is a high percentage – much higher than I would have guessed.

But I try to keep it in proportion. To get 10 to 15 per cent in an exam would be seen as a fairly epic fail. It would mean that you barely registered on the ladder of success.

Incidentally, it pains me to say this, but since the age of 14, I've tried to convince myself that the 14 per cent I got in chemistry at school was okay. (At least I got some of the answers right!)

It was then suggested to me that I reconsider my subject options and swap to art. Test tubes and Bunsen burners were clearly not my strength. No biggie. So, I did change to art and got an A-grade. It was the right decision!

Where MK is concerned, all I can do is carry on with what I'm doing. That means talking to him about how he feels, and being there to hug him tightly, wipe his tears, and kiss his little forehead when he's sad and confused. It means laughing with him when we're doing silly things and when he dances and sings to 'We Will Rock You'.

And at least if he does develop a mental illness, his mummy is in the best possible position to help him understand what he'd be going through, and to hold his hand in battle.

For now though, all I can do is hope against hope that I've not been too generous. That I've not given him the worst gift ever, with no gift receipt and no returns.

CHAPTER 30

MOVING IN THE RIGHT DIRECTION

I'm in my forties now – dangerously close to being on the wrong side of middle-aged – and at times have questioned how on earth I've made it to this age. But I have, and I'm here to tell my tale.

My story is my own, and I have to accept responsibility for all my actions: the good, the bad, and the ugly.

Since I was diagnosed with bipolar, I've learnt so much. I've gradually begun to understand why I behaved in the way that I did when my life was out of control.

Perhaps more importantly though, I've learnt to come to terms with it. I've learnt to believe what others see in me. To believe that the real me is a kind-hearted, compassionate and caring person.

I've come to accept that my behaviour was down to the fact that I was ill. Seriously ill.

Before I was diagnosed, I'd have periods of not recognising the Ali I thought I knew. I'd be horribly confused about what was going on. The gremlin was so forceful and overpowering that I didn't stand a snowball's chance in hell back then.

The thing that troubles me the most though, and has taken me the longest to get over, is the way in which I treated my parents.

We're close. We're incredibly close, and we speak almost every day. And there was never, ever, any doubt about the love between us, but it's been extremely difficult to rid myself of the guilt for the misery I caused.

After hours and hours of therapy and self-reflection, I have learnt to ease up on myself. A bit. I've had to, in order to keep moving forward. If I want to go on working at being a better human being, I can't keep carrying the burdens of the past along with me.

And my parents have given me the greatest gift ... they have forgiven me for my appalling behaviour. Mum, Dad and I reached a beautiful, much anticipated, and very emotionally-charged ceasefire many years ago.

They've done their utmost to gain an understanding of my illness. They never pretend to know what it's really like, they would never be so presumptuous. But they try their very best to put themselves in my shoes. As much as anyone can, without actually experiencing it first-hand, they get it.

There are still too many days when I have to put my positive pants on, plaster on a fake smile, and plough through the mud one more time. Sometimes I doubt whether I have the fight in me. But I guess I must have. I'm still here.

And now? Well, my self-esteem is miles better. It's been a slow and painful process, during which I've had to be completely honest with myself. But I'm getting there.

Like everyone, I will always battle with certain insecurities. I know I'll never be perfect, whatever "perfect" is, but that's okay. And in fact, I don't aspire to be perfect. I'm me.

I do still harbour an unhealthy attitude to food. I go through phases of fasting then feasting. My weight can go up and down like a Singer sewing machine in overdrive. But that's okay too.

I still have OCD tendencies. I mean, I'm not saying I'm a control freak, I just know how to make the bed properly. You can't just go hauling the duvet around with a devil-may-care attitude like some kind of a linen insurgent.

I accept that I have an addictive personality, but I have insight too. I'm aware. And as a result, I can control it.

I'm aware that I still make poor decisions at times, but nothing of any great consequence. Missing three Pilates classes in a two-week period is flaky, but isn't going to harm either me or anyone else.

I never go on wild spending sprees. Gone are the days of inappropriate relationships. (Obviously, now that I'm with Handsome Doc!) And drugs and excessive drinking are a thing of the past, I might add.

When I first made the decision to clean up my life, and to draw a line under drugs and binge drinking, I did find it hard. It was almost like a period of grieving. Those vices had become like friends to me. Clearly, they were not friends. They were destructive and dangerous in so many ways. But I had come to believe that life was better with them.

Some people choose to go into treatment centres for rehab, but I chose to do it myself. The cravings were miserable, and I so nearly buckled on several occasions. But my determination, and the changes I made to my lifestyle, carried me through.

I don't mean to belittle it, because it was really tough. Even when the cravings had subsided, there was the challenge of breaking the habit. Before the decision to abstain, I'd always make sure I was fully stocked up for a night out. What would a night out be like without my little "friend"?

I pulled out of a number of social occasions in those first few months, as I didn't want to put myself in temptation's way. In time though, I felt brighter and ready to embrace my new, clean life. In fact, I almost felt excited. It was like a new dawn.

I barely think about drugs now. The thought still sometimes pops into my mind that it might be fun … just as a one-off …

I can honestly say, though, that the thought lasts all of about five seconds, before I shut it down. I feel panicky at the very mention of it these days. It's a world I no longer wish to be a part of. Life is too good now. It has a purity to it that I don't want to spoil.

Any poor decisions I make now don't affect other people. I do my utmost not to cause hurt and upset. By and large, I'm comfortable with my decision-making process.

I'm close to being comfortable in my own skin. I feel stronger than ever before. And these facets of my personality are okay. They don't stop me from living my life to the full. At least they rarely do.

I now live a life of meaning and substance. I have a responsibility to little MK, and thrive in my role as his mummy. I want to be the best I can be to him. And I want to be the best girlfriend I can to Handsome Doc. Once, those self-inflicted pressures would have felt suffocating. But now, they are the very things to give me a reason to get up in the morning. I am now, finally, able to look forward, rather than stagnate.

I accept that I live with bipolar, and unlike the drink and drug challenges I've overcome, this bipolar thing is unlikely to jog on any time soon. Or any time at all.

But I feel like I'm on the right track.

The experiences in my past are exactly that: in the past. I've been damaged, and I've caused damage, but however dumb and irresponsible some of my actions may have been, they have brought me to where I am today. And that is definitely alright with me.

There will always be hurdles, temptations, and moments of vulnerability, but I know I can cope with almost anything. With continued support and self-awareness, I'll be okay.

CHAPTER 31

COMING CLEAN

Handsome Doc, MK and I have found our groove in our new life together in Surrey.

We're settled, but not in a boring way. We're happy, in a peaceful and contented way.

We've created a home filled with love, joy, respect and support, and it brings the best out in all of us. We have our ups and downs like everyone does, but we know that no problem is insurmountable; together we can get through anything.

We're unbreakable.

As for me? I feel cleansed.

That may sound like an odd thing to say, but it makes sense to me. It's not until relatively recently that I've come clean about my illness. I mean, really come clean. Prior to that, the information was a strictly guarded secret between close friends and family. I was anonymous on Twitter, Instagram and my blog.

Now though, I have set myself free of the burden that I've carried for all these years. The pain of carrying my untold story has gone. I've well and truly come out of my bipolar closet, and it feels good.

Actually, the reason I remained anonymous on social media initially was that, although I wanted to be a mental health advocate, I didn't want it to appear as though it was a self-publicity exercise. I much prefer life away from TV and out of the spotlight, yet I began to feel uncomfortable about my anonymity.

I questioned how I could talk about raising awareness and reducing the stigma by talking about mental health, while hiding behind a pseudonym.

I guess it makes no difference really. Lots of people choose not to reveal their identity and that's absolutely fine. I respect that. The bottom line is that we're all working towards the same thing, but for me, coming clean has been cathartic and rewarding.

It felt right for me to come out. But I know it's not right for everyone.

Throughout my life, prior to receiving an accurate diagnosis and treatment, I made some dreadful decisions. I caused untold hurt and upset. I was stupid and selfish. But I take responsibility for all those times. They were my teacher.

I can't feel regret. There's no point. Regret only serves to keep us from moving forwards. Nor can I change the past. I accept it. Because everything I've done has led me to where I am now.

I've forgiven myself, and have been forgiven by those who matter to me. And most importantly, I can now shape my future.

Mental illness is still such a touchy subject for so many people, and one that often leaves them unsure of what to say. I believe that having reached this stage in my recovery, I have a responsibility to offer support to others who are at a different stage of their journey.

In the past, I was guilty of unhealthy, self-destructive patterns of behaviour. But now, my life is no longer governed by alcohol and drugs. In taking the right meds, monitoring my moods and cleansing myself of my demons, I've reached a place of acceptance and peace. A place where I'm living in the real world along with everybody else.

I'm taking part in life. I'm no longer a spectator of my own existence. I'm an active participant.

I devote much of my time now to raising awareness of mental illness, and to reducing the stigma surrounding it. I'm only one voice, and I don't profess to be able to solve the challenges we face on my own. There are countless other individuals and organisations doing a tremendous job of educating and offering support. But I'd like to think that in my own small way, I'm contributing towards a positive change. At least I hope I am.

I feel confident that, in time, mental illness will be more widely accepted so that people will no longer feel the need to lie about their reasons for needing to take time off work, or for pulling out of social engagements.

But, like everything of substance in life, it will take time.

As for where my journey will take me next?

Who knows!

If you'd asked me 18 months ago where I'd be now, I definitely wouldn't have predicted a life such as the one I'm living. Much as it was what I wanted, I could never in my wildest dreams have believed I could have had that kind of a life.

Finding true love, coming clean about my illness, and in turn discovering a whole new world of support through friends and even social media. Plus, of course, getting my first book published.

But isn't that the beauty of life?

We can make plans, and in some respects we need to, but sometimes, life leads you in a direction you could never have anticipated.

The most important things for me are continued happiness and stability for MK, a happy Handsome Doc, and good health for my nearest and dearest. These things almost go without saying.

Aside from that, I will continue in my role as a mental health advocate. I will continue to expand my network in the field of mental health, in order to give and, when necessary, receive support.

I will continue to write, and I will continue to work on improving my mental wellbeing.

I'm no longer ashamed of my story, and dearly hope that by sharing my journey, and baring my soul, it will help somebody somewhere feel less alone, and more able to heal.

My hope is that, being able to identify with some of the things I've experienced may relieve the painful feeling of isolation for others. Nobody should feel alone. However much bipolar tries to cut us off from the real world, we mustn't let it.

Each of us has built up a strength and resilience to get us through the daily grind of mental illness. I'm a survivor. We all are.

Those illnesses never let us forget our challenges, not for one single day. But we are stronger than our gremlins, and together we can win the fight.

I've discovered that there really is a life worth living, even with bipolar, and will do everything in my power to make it count.

You can too.

ACKNOWLEDGEMENTS

Thank you, Handsome Doc, for putting up with me while I wrote this book. You are my rock and my hero. MK, you give me a reason to fight. Mammy and Doddy, you made me who I am today, and have weathered the storms with courage and love. Waf and Valdo, you've had to put up with too much, but you've shown forgiveness and understanding. Ruby, Dely, Morn, and Jacqu, you've stuck me back together when I've fallen apart and made me laugh when I thought I'd forgotten how to. Shabana, your love, support and honesty mean more to me that you'll ever know, and your incredible journey inspires me to keep travelling mine. Mark, you listen with your heart, and give me the confidence to be myself. Craigie, your gift of fond memories and friendship is so precious. L, your loyalty gives me strength, and your spirit grounds me. Luke, this book wouldn't exist were it not for you.

Thank you all for being part of my journey. And last but by no means least, thank you Chris for helping me to tell my story.

If you found this book interesting ...
why not read these next?

Burlesque or Bust

Bringing My Mental Health To Heel

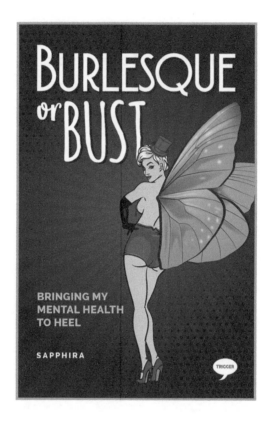

Following a traumatic childhood, Priscilla felt she had lost herself. After a bipolar episode, she threw herself into burlesque dancing and was able to transform from chrysalis to beautiful butterfly – with lots of added sparkle.

Love and Remission

My Life, My Man, My Cancer

Annie Belasco had everything except a man. When she found a lump in her breast, her life seemed to topple over. But though she was facing mortality at such a young age, she didn't let it stop her from finding love ... and remission.

Searching for Brighter Days

Learning to Manage my Bipolar Brain

Searching for Brighter Days traces Karen Manton's journey through the extreme highs and lows she felt in her life before she was diagnosed with bipolar disorder and began to learn how to manage her life.

the *Shaw* mind
FOUNDATION

Creating hope for children,
adults and families

Sign up to our charity, The Shaw Mind Foundation
www.shawmindfoundation.org
and keep in touch with us; we would love to hear
from you.

*We aim to bring to an end the suffering and despair caused
by mental health issues. Our goal is to make help and support
available for every single person in society, from all walks of
life. We will never stop offering hope. These are our promises.*

www.triggerpublishing.com

Trigger is a publishing house devoted to opening conversations about mental health. We tell the stories of people who have suffered from mental illnesses and recovered, so that others may learn from them.

Adam Shaw is a worldwide mental health advocate and philanthropist. Now in recovery from mental health issues, he is committed to helping others suffering from debilitating mental health issues through the global charity he co-founded, The Shaw Mind Foundation. www.shawmindfoundation.org

Lauren Callaghan (CPsychol, PGDipClinPsych, PgCert, MA (hons), LLB (hons), BA), born and educated in New Zealand, is an innovative industry-leading psychologist based in London, United Kingdom. Lauren has worked with children and young people, and their families, in a number of clinical settings providing evidence based treatments for a range of illnesses, including anxiety and obsessional problems. She was a psychologist at the specialist national treatment centres for severe obsessional problems in the UK and is renowned as an expert in the field of mental health, recognised for diagnosing and successfully treating OCD and anxiety related illnesses in particular. In addition to appearing as a treating clinician in the critically acclaimed and BAFTA award-winning documentary *Bedlam*, Lauren is a frequent guest speaker on mental health conditions in the media and at academic conferences. Lauren also acts as a guest lecturer and honorary researcher at the Institute of Psychiatry Kings College, UCL.

Please visit the link below:

www.triggerpublishing.com

Join us and follow us...

@triggerpub

Search for us on Facebook